# UGLY KID JOE

## AMERICA'S LEAST WANTED

Midori Tsukagoshi

Management: Dennis Rider for Rider Management
Transcribed by Paul Pappas, Steve Gorenberg
Kerry O'Brien, Jon Chappell and Mark Phillips
Music Engraving by W.R. Music
Production Manager: Daniel Rosenbaum
Art Direction: Rosemary Cappa
Director Of Music: Mark Phillips

*Cover illustration by Moish Brenman*

ISBN: 089524-732-1

# CONTENTS

# TABLATURE EXPLANATION

**TABLATURE:** A six-line staff that graphically represents the guitar fingerboard, with the top line indicating the highest sounding string (high E). By placing a number on the appropriate line, the string and fret of any note can be indicated. The number 0 represents an open string.

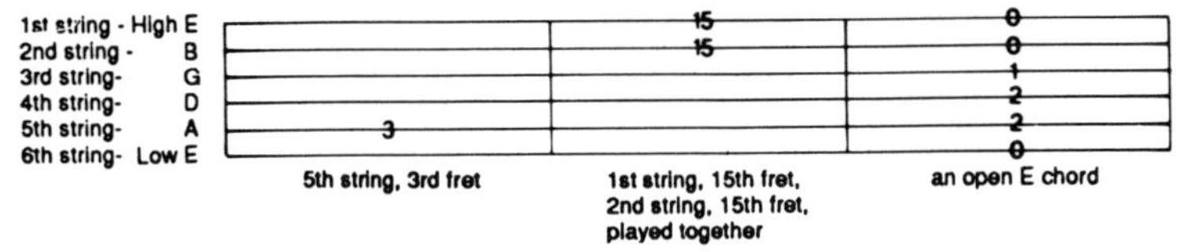


## Definitions for Special Guitar Notation

**BEND:** Strike the note and bend up ½ step (one fret).

**BEND:** Strike the note and bend up a whole step (two frets).

**BEND AND RELEASE:** Strike the note and bend up ½ (or whole) step, then release the bend back to the original note. All three notes are tied, only the first note is struck.

**PRE-BEND:** Bend the note up ½ (or whole) step, then strike it.

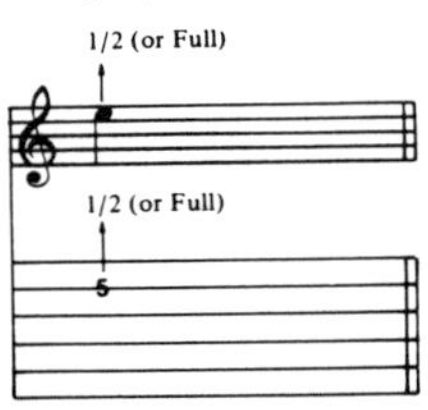


**PRE-BEND AND RELEASE:** Bend the note up ½ (or whole) step. Strike it and release the bend back to the original note.

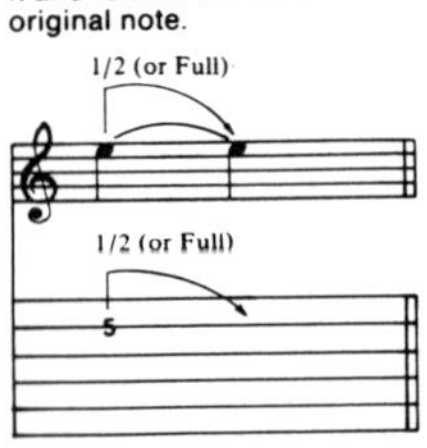


**UNISON BEND:** Strike the two notes simultaneously and bend the lower note up to the pitch of the higher.

**VIBRATO:** The string is vibrated by rapidly bending and releasing the note with the left hand or tremolo bar.

**WIDE OR EXAGGERATED VIBRATO:** The pitch is varied to a greater degree by vibrating with the left hand or tremolo bar.

**SLIDE:** Strike the first note and then slide the same left-hand finger up or down to the second note. The second note is not struck.

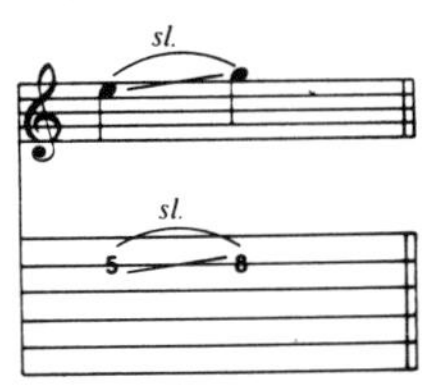


**SLIDE:** Same as above, except the second note is struck.

**HAMMER-ON:** Strike the first (lower) note, then sound the higher note with another finger by fretting it without picking.

**PULL-OFF:** Place both fingers on the notes to be sounded. Strike the first note and without picking, pull the finger off to sound the second (lower) note.

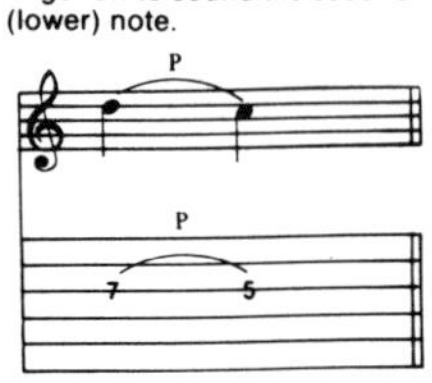


**TRILL:** Very rapidly alternate between the note indicated and the small note shown in parentheses by hammering on and pulling off.

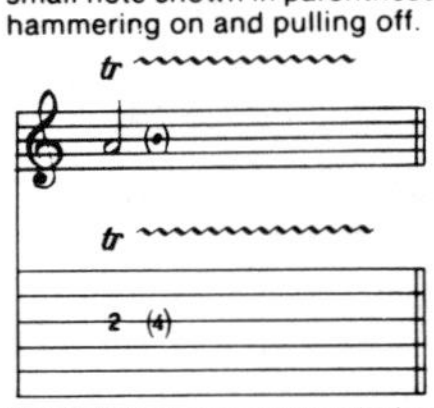

**TAPPING:** Hammer ("tap") the fret indicated with the right-hand index or middle finger and pull off to the note fretted by the left hand.

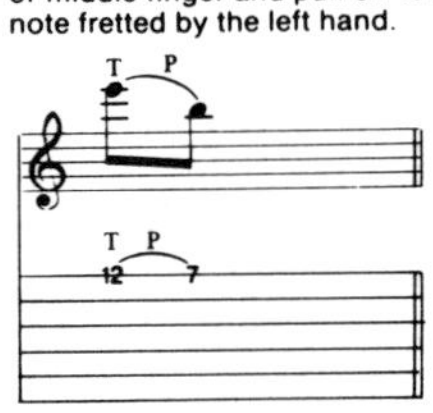


**PICK SLIDE:** The edge of the pick is rubbed down the length of the string producing a scratchy sound.

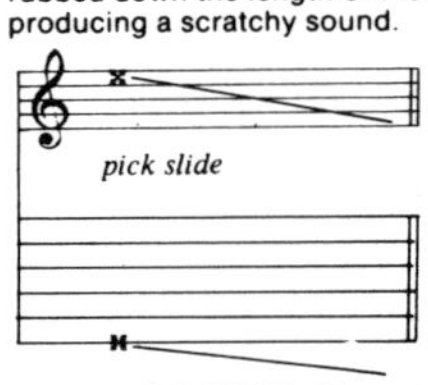


**TREMOLO PICKING:** The note is picked as rapidly and continuously as possible.

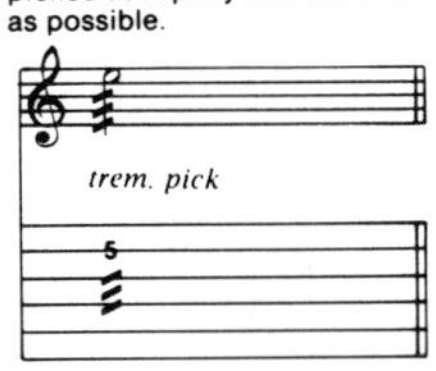


**NATURAL HARMONIC:** Strike the note while the left hand lightly touches the string over the fret indicated.

**ARTIFICIAL HARMONIC:** The note is fretted normally and a harmonic is produced by adding the edge of the thumb or the tip of the index finger of the right hand to the normal pick attack. High volume or distortion will allow for a greater variety of harmonics.

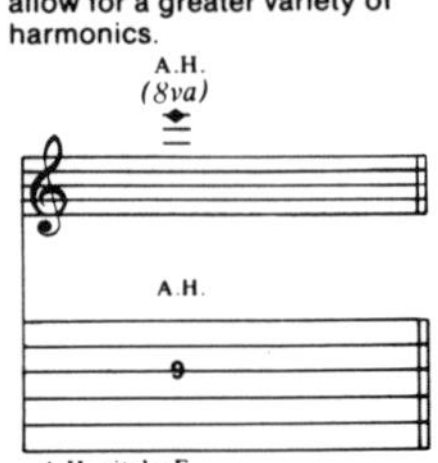


A.H. pitch: E

**TREMOLO BAR:** The pitch of the note or chord is dropped a specified number of steps then returned to the original pitch.

**PALM MUTING:** The note is partially muted by the right hand lightly touching the string(s) just before the bridge.

**MUFFLED STRINGS:** A percussive sound is produced by laying the left hand across the strings without depressing them and striking them with the right hand.

**RHYTHM SLASHES:** Strum chords in rhythm indicated. Use chord voicings found in the fingering diagrams at the top of the first page of the transcription.

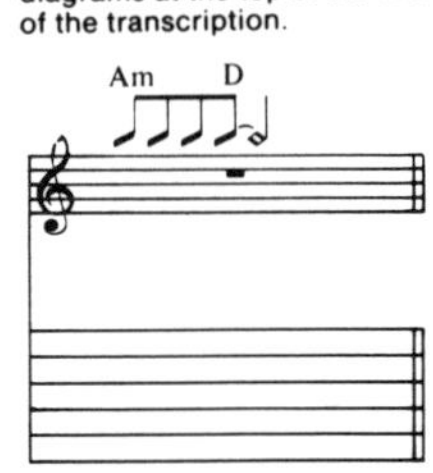


**RHYTHM SLASHES (SINGLE NOTES):** Single notes can be indicated in rhythm slashes. The circled number above the note name indicates which string to play. When successive notes are played on the same string, only the fret numbers are given.

# Neighbor

Words and Music by
Ugly Kid Joe

1st, 2nd Verses
G5 B♭5 F5 G5 B♭5 F5 G5 B♭5 F5
1. Sit - tin' in your front yard drink - ing lem - on - ade.
2. See additional lyrics
Gtrs. IV & V
P.M.
G5 B♭5 N.C. G5 B♭5 F5 G5 B♭5 F5
Sub - ur - ban life, a pret - ty wife, you
G5 B♭5 F5 2nd time w/Fill 1 G5 B♭5 B5 C5 E♭5 B♭5
think you got it made. But, you don't know what's
Fill 1 (Gtr. I)
A.H. Full
(15ma)
A.H. pitch: G

2nd time Gtr. IV substitute Rhy. Fill 1
(cont. in notation)
C5 E♭5 B♭5 C5 E♭5 B♭5 C5 A E♭5 A F5III A
Gtr. V
P.M.
— in store — for you and your fam - i - ly. — Ha, ha, I'm
(Gtr. V cont. in slashes)
Gtr. IV sl.
G5 B♭5 F5 G5 B♭5 F5 G5 B♭5 F5
mov - in' in, — right next door. — Won't you wel - come me? —
Gtrs. IV & V
(Gtr. V cont. in slashes)
1.
G5 E B♭5 A C5 D♭5
Half-time feel
Chorus
D5
(cont. in notation)
— It's a beau - ti - ful day — in the neigh - bor - hood. — And I
Gtr. IV
Rhy. Fill 1 (Gtr. IV)

(end half time feel)
C5 D5 B♭5 N.C. G5 B♭5 F5
hope I did - n't ru - in your day. Wont you be my neigh - bor?
Gtrs. IV & V
P.M. sl. P.M. P.M. P.M. P.M.
G5 B♭5 F5 G5 B♭5 F5 N.C.
2. Yeah, I
A.H. (15ma)
P.M. P.M. P.M. H sl.
A.H. pitch: F
2.
Gtr. V
G5 ⑥ open E B♭5 ⑤ open A C5 D♭5
Half time feel
Chorus
D5
It's a beau - ti - ful day in the neigh - bor - hood. And
Gtr. IV
P.M.
C5
(cont. in notation)
D5 C5
if I could I sure - ly would in - vite you in and say,
Gtrs. IV & V
P.M. P.M.

N.C.
G5
G Gsus4
C7
"Won't you be my neigh - bor?
Whispered: (Won't you be)
Uh, won't you be my neigh - bor?
Uh, won't you be my neigh - bor?
Uh, could you be my neigh - bor?
(end half time feel)
Uh, won't you be my neigh - bor?
Uh, come on, I don't think you'll find a place to live in peace
Uh, won't you be my neigh - bor?
H
let ring
f

G5 GGsus4 C7 G5 G Gsus4 C7
of mind. You're gon - na live in mis - er - y. Uh, when you're liv - in' next
Uh, won't you be my neigh - bor? Uh, won't you be my neigh - bor?"
let ring
H
Half-time feel
Chorus
B7 C7 N.C. C7 Db7 D7
to me. It's a beau - ti - ful day in the neigh - bor - hood. Raaah!
(Gtr. V cont. in slashes) Gtr. IV
(cont. in notation)
(end half-time feel)
Guitar solo I
C5 C7 N.C. G5 E Bb5 E F5 E
Gtrs. IV & V
P.M.
Won't you be my, won't you be my funk - y neigh-bor, neigh - bor?
Gtrs. IV & V
(cont. in slashes)
Gtr. I
Full

G5 E B♭5 E F5 E G5 E B♭5 E F5 E G5 E B♭5 A B♭5 B5
P.M.
A.H.
(15ma)
Full
H P
sl.
C5 A E♭5 A B♭5 A C5 A E♭5 A B♭5 A G5 E B♭5 E F5 E
G5 E B♭5 A C5 D♭5 D5
C5 E F F♯ G5 E B♭5 E F5 E
open
1fr.
2fr.

G5 E B♭5 E F5 E G5 E B♭5 E F5 E
⑥ open
P.M.
Full
sl
P H P H P
H P
(Gtr. IV cont. in Rhy. Fill 2)
⑥3fr.
G C5 D♭5 D5
Freely (♩ = 84)
w/Rhy. Fill 2
Gtr. V
(cont. in notation)
A.H.
(8va)
(Gtr. I out)
In time ♩ = 100
N.C.
A.H. pitch: F♯
*Gtr V fades in & out and pans back & forth from left to right next 4 bars.
w/spitting & belching
Well, I drink,
Gtr. VI
Rhy. Fill 2 (Gtr. IV)
(Gtr. IV out)

A Little Faster ♩ = 108
Half-time feel
w/Rhy. Fill 3
G13
C7
and I stink. I
*grad. accel.
Gtr. VI
mf let ring
let ring
clean tone
*grad. accel.
*grad. accel.
**w/slide
mf
*Next 27 bars.
**Next 8 bars.
G7
w/coughing
C7
w/laughing
smoke, I'm a joke. I
let ring
let ring
(Gtr. V out)
Rhy. Fill 3
(Gtr. IV)
let ring
w/clean tone
let ring
let ring
(Gtr. IV out)

G7
C7
try all night and day to get a piece of the ac - tion, a - ha. And
let ring
let ring
G7
C7
(end half time feel)
you should know by now you're nev- er gon-na for - get, a - ha. Well I know
let ring
G7
w/Fill 2
C7
G7
C7
just what you're think - ing. It could be you out 'n' you're drink - in'. Don't you knock
Fill 2 (Gtr. V)
1.
2.
(cont. in notation)
H P P P P
H P P
P.M.
H P P P P
H P P

Gtr. G5
IV
⑤3fr.
C
(cont. in notation)
P.M.
it un - til you try___ it. It could be you in a lit - tle while.__
(Ooh, while.)
*Vol. knob swell.
C7 B7 C7 D♭7 D7 C7
I hope I did - n't ru - in your day. Ow!
Gtrs. IV, V & VI
(Gtr. VI out)
Gtrs. IV & V
trem. bar
*Depress bar before striking note.
Moderate Rock ♩ = 138
Guitar solo II
w/Rhy. Fig. 1 (15 times)
G5 E B♭5 E F5 E G5 E B♭5 E F5 E G5 E B♭5 E F5 E
Gtr. I
sl.

G5 E B♭5 E F5 E
⑥ open
Full
1/2
P
H
sl.
w/Fills 3 & 3A
Gtrs. I & II
Gtr. II
w/Fill 3A
Fill 3 (Gtr. III)
Fill 3A (Gtr. I)

Half-time feel
Chorus
w/Fill 4
G5 B♭5 C5 D♭5 D5
Gtr. V
It's a beau - ti - ful day in the neigh - bor - hood. And I
Full
Gtrs. I, II & III
Gtrs. IV & V
(Gtr. V cont. in slashes)
Gtr. IV
P.M.
C5 D5
dig your wife, she sure is good. A beau - ti - ful day in the neigh -
Fill 4 (Gtr. III)
P P

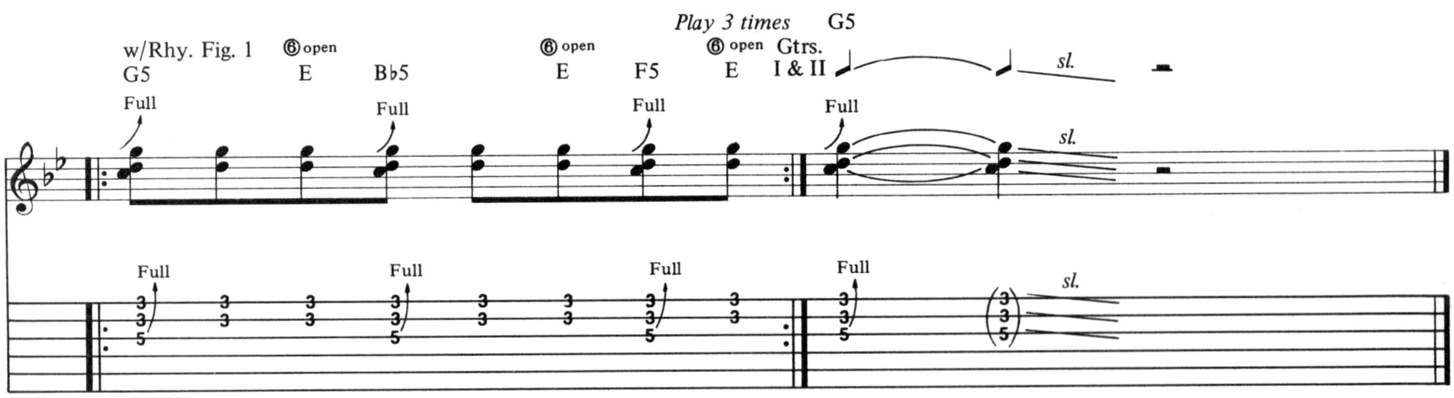


*Additional Lyrics*

2. I brought my life, my ugly wife, my dirty dog with fleas.
My kid's a punk and I'm a drunk, but this I'm sure you'll see.
And you don't know what it's like to live in misery.
Come on and welcome to home sweet hell, dissatisfaction guaranteed.
*(To Chorus)*

# Goddamn Devil

Words and Music by
Ugly Kid Joe

Half time feel
1st, 2nd Verses
E5 E5(7) Asus4 A E5 E5(7)
1. Rape, D. U. I., as - sault___ and bat - ter - y. These are the things that will
2. I know the sto - ry a - bout your life,___ if you killed your broth - er or you
(Gtr. II out)
trem. bar
dim.
*Play 1st time only (next 2 bars).
a tempo
let ring
let ring
sim.
Asus4 A E5 E5(7) Asus4 A
bring you to me.___ Mur - der and theft and all___ of the a - bove. You can
beat your wife.___ And I am here to pun - ish you.___

1st time w/Fill 1
E5
E5(7)
Asus4
(end half time feel)
A
E5
E5(7)
bet your life I know what you're think - in' of.
you can't fool me 'cause I ain't no fool.
I've tak - en you and I'll
The time has come to
(Gtr. I out) Gtr. III
Gtr. III
P.M.
Asus4
A
E5
E5(7)
Asus4
A5
take your friends.
say good - bye.
Don't you wor - ry, we'll all meet in the end.
The end is here for those who cheat, steal and lie.
'Cause
P.M.
E5
E5(7)
Asus4
A
E5
E5(7)
life's a bitch and then you die.
There will be tor - ture and there will be pain.
Trust me, ba - by, 'cause
'Cause this is hell, ba - by,
P.M.
Fill 1
Gtr. II

Chorus
Asus4 A5 E5 G5 A5 D5 A5 G5
I don't lie.
die in flames.
I'm the God - damn
Rhy. Fig. 2
P.M. sl.
*w/Rhy. Fig. 2 (2½ times)
E5 G5 A5 D5 A5 G5 E5 G5 A5 D5 A5 G5 E5 G5 A5
Dev - il. This job pleas - es me. I'm the God - damn Dev - il,
*2nd time play 6½ times.
1.
E5 E5(7) Asus4 A E5 E5(7) Asus4 A
and I do it for free.
(Gtr. III out)
Gtr. I
mf let ring let ring sim.
2.
D5 A5 G5 E5 G5 A5 D5 A5 G5 E5 G5 A5
Sa - tan if you please. I'm the God - damn Dev - il.
D5 A5 G5 E5 G5 A5 D5 A5 G5 E5 G5 A5
This job pleas - es me. I'm the God - damn Dev - il,

E5
E5(7)
w/Fill 2
E5
and I do it for free.
(Gtr. III out)
Gtr. I
mf let ring
sim.
Faster ♩ = 170
Bridge
F♯5
B5
F♯5
I don't care a-bout you, don't care a-bout your life.
(Gtr. I out)
Gtr. III
Gtr. III
f
sl.
P.M.
P
B5
C5
F♯5
B5
Don't care a-bout your chil-dren or
Fill 2
Gtr. II

F♯5
B5
C5
F♯5
A5
B5
all a - bout your wife.
I'm here to do my job,
A.H.
(15ma)
P.M.
sl.
A.H. pitch: G
so if you broke the law,
you're
P
check - in' in with me,
but you can nev - er leave.
Tempo I
Half time feel
3rd Verse
E5
E5(7)
There's one way out, but
(Gtr. III out)
Gtr. I
mf
let ring

Asus4 A E5 E5(7) Asus4 A
(end half time feel)
if you dare, we'll make a deal: you'll grow your hair; as
(Gtr. I out)
sim.
Gtr. III
E5 E5(7) Asus4 A E5 E5(7) Asus4 A
Sa-tan's child, you'll start a band and spread the word a-cross the land!
Gtr. II
8va
trem. bar
Gtr. III
P.M.
Guitar solo
w/Rhy. Fig. 2 (8 times)
E5 G5 A5 D5 A5 G5
I'm the God-damn
Gtr. II
Full
H P

E5 G5 A5 D5 A5 G5
Oh!
Dev - il.
E5 G5 A5 D5 A5 G5 E5 G5 A5
I'm the God - damn Dev - il.
A.H. pitches: F♯
G
A.H. pitches: E
C♯
D5 A5 G5 E5 G5 A5 D5 A5 G5
I'm the God - damn
semi-harm.
trem. bar
*Depress bar before striking note.
E5 G5 A5 D5 A5 G5
Dev - il.

E5 G5 A5 D5 A5 G5
I'm the God - damn
A.H. (15ma) Full P
A.H. (15ma) H H
A.H. pitches: F♯
F♯
E E E
E5 G5 A5 D5 A5 G5
Dev - il.
8va
H H P H P
grad. bend
Chorus
w/Rhy. Fig. 2 (3½ times)
E5 G5 A5 D5 A5 G5 E5 G5 A5
I'm the God - damn Dev - il.
(I'm the God - damn Dev - il, Dev - il, the
8va
(Gtr. II out)
dim.

D5 A5 G5 E5 G5 A5
This job pleas - es me.
Dev - il.
D5 A5 G5 E5 G5 A5
I'm the God - damn Dev - il,
I'm the God - damn Dev - il, the Dev - il, the
N.C. E5 G5 A5 D5 A5 G5
Sa - tan if you please.
Dev - il.
I'm the God - damn
I'm the God - damn
Rhy. Fig. 2A
P.M.
sl.
w/Rhy. Fig. 2A (2 times)
E5 G5 A5 D5 A5 G5 E5 G5 A5 D5 A5 G5
Dev il. Bet - ter be - lieve in me, on - ly me. I'm the God - damn
Dev il.) (I'm the God - damn
E5 G5 A5 G5 E5
Outro
w/Rhy. Fig. 1 (3¾ times)
E5(7)
Dev - il.
Dev - il, the Dev - il, the Dev - il.)
Gtr. II
Full
mf
*Let sustain for next 8 bars.

Asus4
A
E5
E5(7)
Oh!
Full
*w/devilish laughter
Ooh, sweet Sa - tan, ooh,
I be - lieve in... me.
N.C.
w/laughter
Gtr. II
Gtr. I
rit.
*Next 9 bars.
*Gtr. II indicated to left of slashes in tab.

# Come Tomorrow

Words and Music by
Ugly Kid Joe and Roger Lahr

E7#9 A7 G7 N.C. E7#9 G7 A7 N.C. E7#9 A7 G7 N.C.
met the dev - il, kept my soul. Walk - in' out on lakes of fire and I'm gone.
E7#9 G7 A7 N.C. E7#9 A7 G7 N.C.
Walk - in' in a won - der - land, I don't real - ly un - der - stand the
E7#9 G7 A7 N.C. E7#9 A7 G7 N.C.
place I'm com - ing to right now to - day.
*Gtrs. IV & V
Chorus
F#5 A5 ⑥3fr. G F#5
Come to - mor - row, you could see the light. Come to - mor - row,
Rhy. Fig. 2 (Gtrs. I & III)
let ring
*Gtrs. IV & V w/distortion.
w/Fill 1
A5
(Gtrs. IV & V out)
w/Rhy. Figs. 1 & 1A (both 2 times)
N.C. E7#9 G7 A7 N.C.
break it right down to the place you were be - fore. Yeah.
Gtr. II
(end Rhy. Fig. 2)
1/2
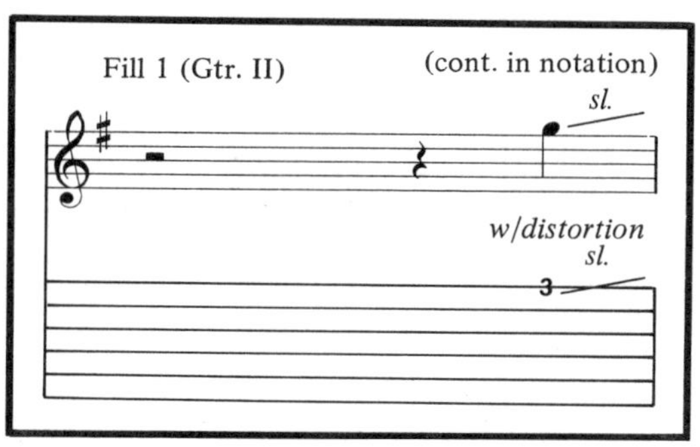
Fill 1 (Gtr. II)
(cont. in notation)
sl.
w/distortion
sl.

E7♯9 A7 G7 N.C. E7♯9 G7 A7 N.C. E7♯9 A7 G7 N.C.
(Spoken:) Yeah, come on.
Well,
2nd Verse
w/Rhy. Figs. 1 (Gtrs. I & IV)
& 1A (Gtrs. III & V) (both times)
E7♯9 G7 A7 N.C. E7♯9 A7 G7 N.C. E7♯9 G7 A7 N.C.
fif - teen years on down_the line,_ I guess you'd say I'm do - in' fine._ Wan - der - ing down that same_ old road a - gain._
E7♯9 A7 G7 N.C. E7♯9 G7 A7 N.C. E7♯9 A7 G7 N.C.
A - walk - in' in her won - der - land,_ but Al - ice does - n't un - der - stand_ the
E7♯9 G7 A7 N.C. E7♯9 A7 G7 N.C.
place she's com - in' to_ right now to - day._ O - kay,_ yeah._
(cont. in Fill 2)

Chorus
w/Rhy. Fig. 2
w/Fill 2
F♯7add4
w/Fill 3
Aadd2
Come to - mor - row, you could see the light.
Rhy. Fig. 2A (Gtrs. IV & V)
P.M.
F♯7add4
A
Come to - mor - row, I think you break it right down to the place that you were be - fore.
(end Rhy. Fig. 2A)
sl.
N.C.(E5)
Yeah, yeah, yeah, be - fore. Come on,
Rhy. Fig. 3
P.M.
P
Fill 2 (Gtr. II)
Fill 3 (Gtr. VI)
steady gliss.
w/slide

w/Fill 4
Bridge
(F♯5)
come on, come on, come on.
Move a lit - tle slow - er.
P.M.
P
(A5)
Ya come a lit - tle fast - er, hon - ey.
On your knees, you'll be beg - gin' me please. As you
sl.
Guitar solo
w/Rhy. Figs. 1 (Gtr. IV)
& 1A (Gtr. V) (both 4 times)
(B5)
D5
D♯5
N.C.
E7♯9
G7
A7
feel the dis - ease, you're go - in' down a - gain to - night.
Gtr. II
Gtr. IV
Gtr. V
1/2
Full
Fill 4 (Gtr. VI)
w/slide

E7♯9
A7
G7
N.C.
A.H.
(8va)
1/2
Full
1/4
P
H
sl.
A.H. pitch: B
A.H. pitches: B
E5
F5
F♯5
Ah.
(15ma)
Gtrs. IV & V
P.M.

F♯5
G♯5
A5
B♭5
Ah.
Ah.
A.H.
(15ma)
Full
A.H.
(15ma)
sl.
1/2
P.M.
A.H. pitches: F♯ F♯ E E
B5
D5
D♯5
H P
sl.
trem. bar
12
3
6

w/Rhy. Fig. 1 (2 times)
E5 E7♯9 G7 A7 N.C. E7♯9 A7 G7 N.C. E7♯9 G7 A7 N.C.
Full
H P P H P
mf
Full P
(Gtrs. IV & V out)
w/Rhy. Fill 1
E7♯9 A7 G7 N.C.
3rd Verse
w/Rhy. Fig. 1 (4 times)
E7♯9 G7 A7 N.C. E7♯9 A7 G7 N.C.
(Spoken:) Yeah, yeah.
See me run-nin', watch me fall. I guess you'd say I've fi-n'ly found my own.
sl.
Rhy. Fill 1 (Gtr. III)
(cont. in Rhy. Fig. 1A)
sl.
P

w/Rhy. Fig. 1A (3 times)
E7♯9 G7 A7 N.C. E7♯9 A7 G7 N.C. E7♯9 G7 A7 N.C.
Yeah, yeah. See me cry - in' and won - der why. I
sl.
w/Rhy. Fill 2
E7♯9 A7 G7 N.C. E7♯9 G7 A7 N.C. E7♯9 A7 G7 N.C.
guess you'd say it's time to die to - day, o - kay, o - kay, o - kay, yeah, yeah.
Chorus
w/Rhy. Figs. 2 & 2A
F♯7add4 Aadd2
Now, come to - mor - row, well, you could see the light, uh.

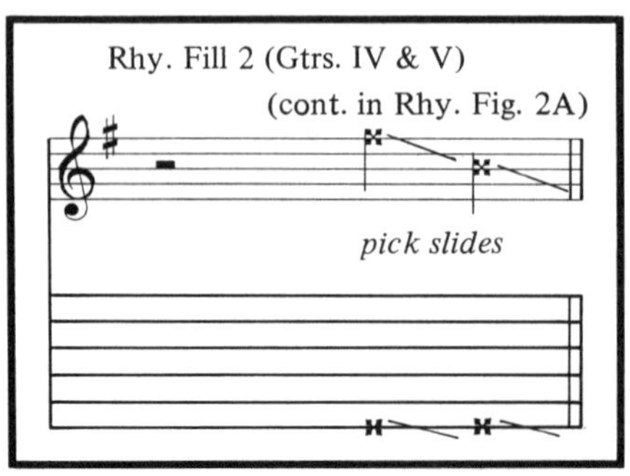
Rhy. Fill 2 (Gtrs. IV & V)
(cont. in Rhy. Fig. 2A)
pick slides

F♯7add4
w/Rhy. Fill 3
A
w/Rhy. Fig. 3 (4 times)
N.C.(E5)
Now come to - mor - row, I think ya break it right down to the place that you were be - fore.
Yeah, now. Mm, be - fore. I said, ah. Come on.
Full
P
Outro
w/Rhy. Fig. 3 (11 times)
N.C.(E5)
Full
1/2
P H P
Full
P
Full
1/2

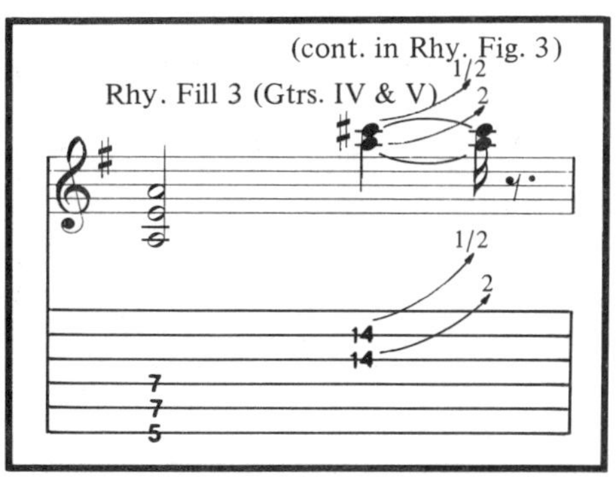
(cont. in Rhy. Fig. 3)
Rhy. Fill 3 (Gtrs. IV & V)
1/2
2

w/Rhy. Fig. 3A
(cont. in Fill 5)
Rhy. Fig. 3A (Gtr. VI)
Play 7 times
P.M.

w/Fill 5
E13
Uh, hi,— hi,— oh.— Hi,— hi,—
Gtrs. I & III
let ring-
H H
Gtrs. IV & V
1/2 1/2
E5
oh.— Hi,— hi,— oh.
let ring-
H H
1/2 1/2
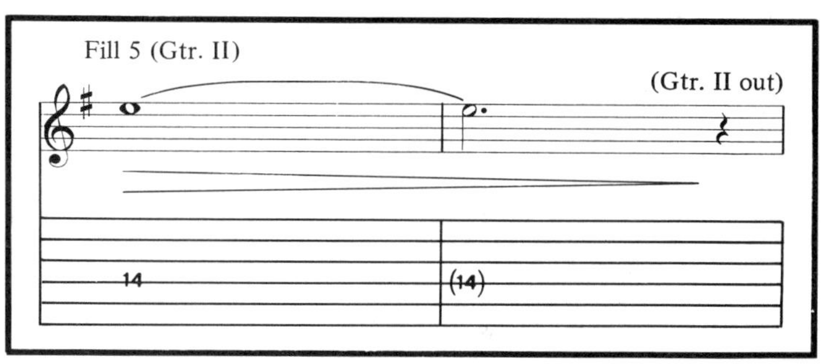
Fill 5 (Gtr. II)
(Gtr. II out)

# Panhandlin' Prince

Words and Music by
Ugly Kid Joe

F♯5 G5
sl.
Smoke cig-a-rettes and drink my Mick-ey's fine malt liq-uor brew. As I
Fdbk. 1/2
(8va)
grad. accel.
start drink-in', and I start think-in' that death is on my side. Well, if my
C5 B♭5
(Gtr. III out)
Gtrs. I & II
Faster ♩ = 138
G5
heart stopped beat-in', the street kept reek-in', that's su - i - cide. (That's right.)
Rhy. Fig. 1
(end Rhy. Fig. 1)
P.M.

F♯5 G5
Rhy. Fig. 2
B♭5
F♯5 G5
P.M.
sl.
w/Fill 1
C5
B♭5
(end Rhy. Fig. 2)
w/Rhy. Fig. 2
F♯5 G5
Gtr. III
Full
1/2
A.H.
(15ma)
A.H. pitches: G F A♭
F♯5 G5
C5
B♭5
(Gtr. III out)
P

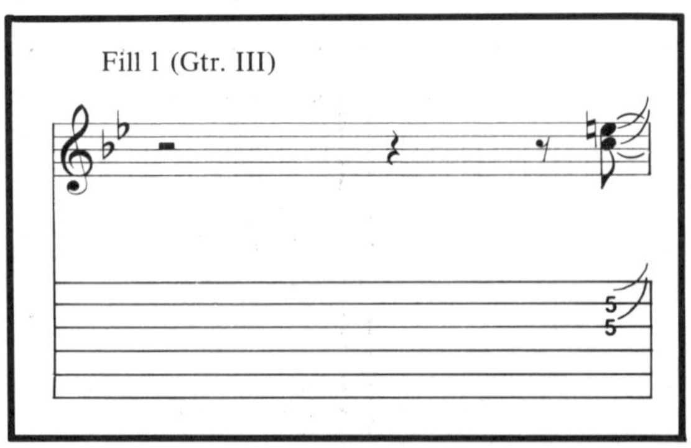
Fill 1 (Gtr. III)

2nd, 3rd Verses
w/Rhy. Fig. 2
F♯5 G5
B♭5
F♯5 G5
C5 B♭5
2. I grew up in the in - ner cit - y, a dark part of this town.
3. See additional lyrics
w/Rhy. Fig. 2 (1st 3 bars only)
F♯5 G5
B♭5
2nd time w/Fill 3
F♯5 G5
w/Rhy. Fill 1
w/Fill 2 (1st time only)
C5 B♭5
Just an - oth - er in - no - cent back woods vic - tim, so - ci - e - ty like to put down. You can call
w/Rhy. Fig. 2
F♯5 G5
B♭5
F♯5 G5
C5
B♭5
me a booz - er, call me a los - er, real - ly does - n't mat - ter to me. I got a
w/Rhy. Fig. 1
G5
C5
B♭5
G5
bench for snooz - in', some sauce to keep booz - in'. That's all I need. I said,

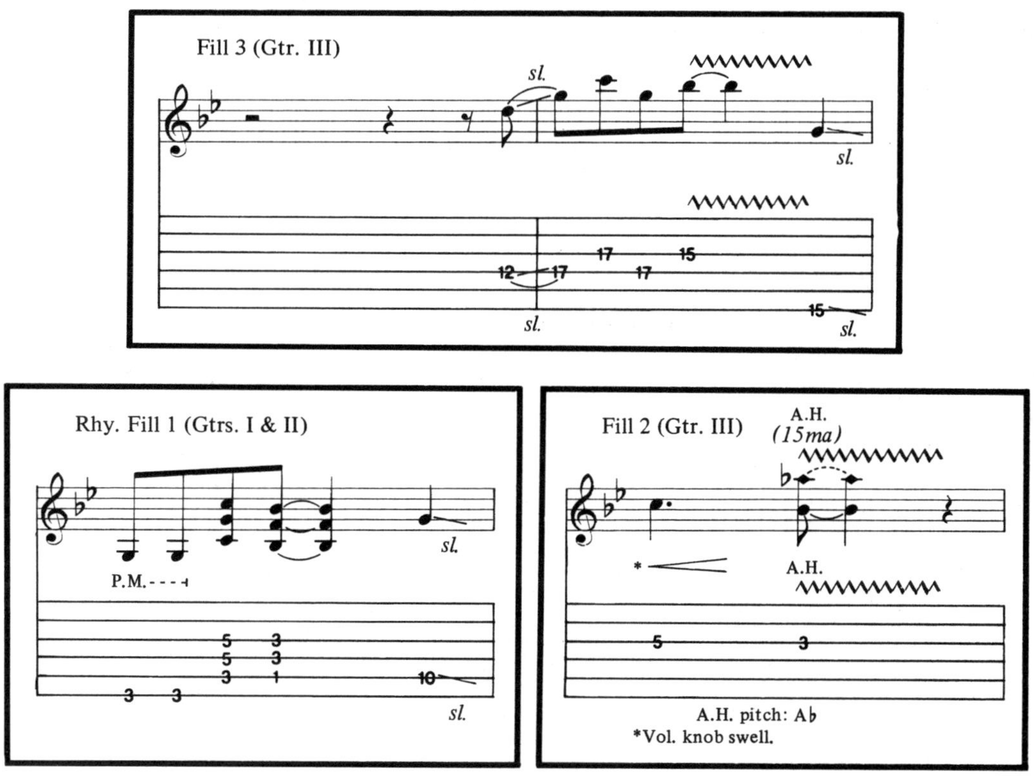
Fill 3 (Gtr. III)
sl.
Rhy. Fill 1 (Gtrs. I & II)
P.M.
sl.
Fill 2 (Gtr. III)
A.H.
(15ma)
A.H.
A.H. pitch: A♭
*Vol. knob swell.

*Vol. knob swell.

2.
w/Rhy. Fills 2 & 2A
F5 C5 Bb5 G5 N.C.
w/Rhy. Figs. 3 & 3A
G5 Bb
the day I die, good - bye.
I keep it com - in', some-
C5 Bb5 G5 N.C. G5 Bb5
times don't know why.
Ooh yeah, I'm gon - na do it un - til
F5 F#5 G5 N.C.
4th Verse
F#5 G5 F#5 G5 Bb5
the day I die.
4. Yo, Mis - ter Trump, can I ask you a ques - tion? You got
Gtrs. I & II
A.H.
(8va)
H
sl.
P.M.
A.H. pitches: G Ab G F
Gtr. IV
Rhy. Fill 2 (Gtrs. I & II)
Rhy. Fill 2A (Gtr. IV)

F♯5 G5 F♯5 G5 C5 F♯5G5 F♯5 G5 B♭5
some spare change for me, suck - er? Now I'm down and out, and there ain't no doubt that
sl.
P.M.
let ring
F♯5 G5 N.C.(C) C♯°7 F♯5 G5
I am here to stay. Yeah, you see me with my broth - ers, ly - in'
sl.
(Gtr. IV out) Gtr. III
1/2

F♯5 G5 B♭5
F♯5 G5
F♯5 G5 C5
in the gut-ter with my, my pa-per bag in hand. Yeah, the streets
sl.
P.M.
Full
F♯5 G5
F♯5 G5 B♭5
C5 B♭5 G5
are cold, but at least there's soul, all I need.
(cont. in slashes)
1/2
Full
Fdbk.
H

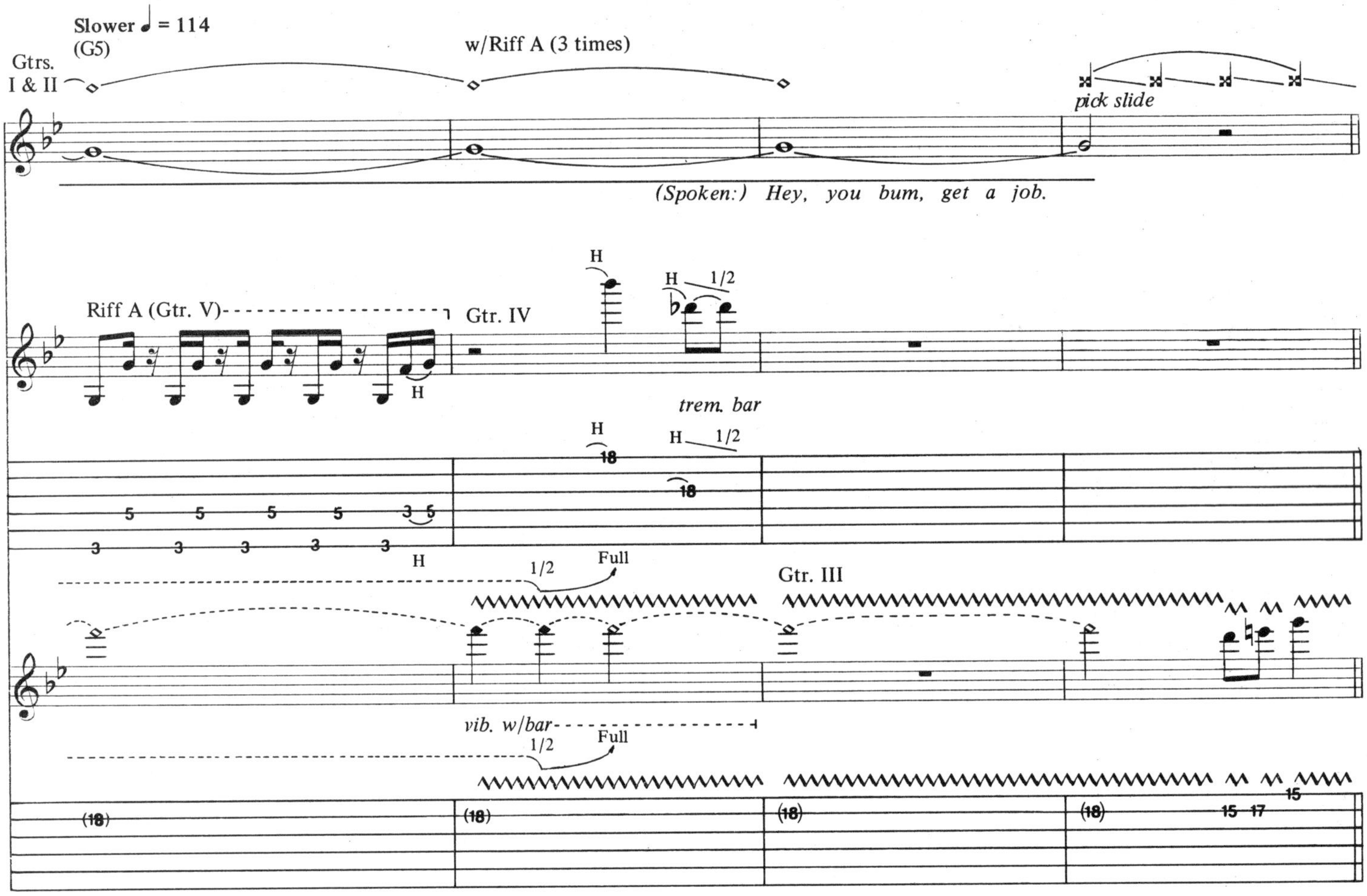
Slower ♩ = 114
(G5)
w/Riff A (3 times)
Gtrs. I & II
pick slide
(Spoken:) Hey, you bum, get a job.
Riff A (Gtr. V)
Gtr. IV
trem. bar
vib. w/bar
Gtr. III

Bridge
w/Riff A (14 times) & Rhy. Fig. 4
B♭5
C5
You'll take a - way my peace of mind. You'll leave me there to rot and die.
(Gtr. III)

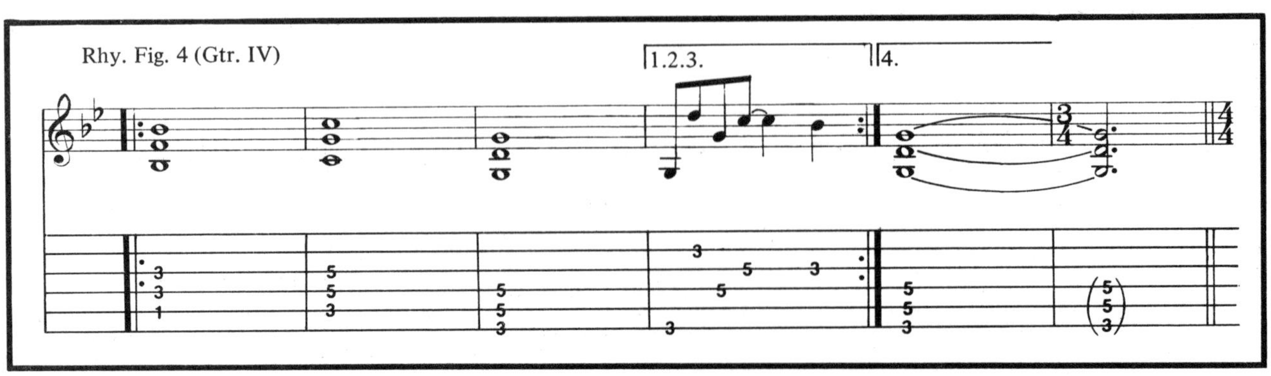
Rhy. Fig. 4 (Gtr. IV)
1.2.3.
4.

G5
*(Die.) Yeah, yeah.
*Echo repeat.
Full
Bb5
C5
But look a-gain, my care-less friend. The world you live is just a
w/Fill 4
G5
Bb5
lie. Yeah. It's give and take, the more the fake,
Fill 4** (Gtr. VI)
**Two gtrs. arr. for one gtr.
*Vol. knob swells.

C5
G5
the more the pain, the more you lose.
Yeah, yeah, yeah, yeah.
Full
sl.
Bb5
C5
Gtrs. I, II & V
G5
(Gtr. V out)
So live your life, don't take no sides, 'n' seize the day, and drink your booze. * (Booze, booze, booze, booze.)
* Echo repeats.
(Gtr. III out)
P
Faster ♩ = 122
Double-time feel
N.C.
Gtr. I
H
Riff B (Gtr. II)
(end Riff B)

1.
H
2.
Gtr. III
Gtr. I
sl.
Gtrs. I & II
Guitar solo
B♭5
C5
A.H.
(15ma)
Gtr. III
Gtr. I
w/Riff B
G5
Full
A.H. pitches: F E F F G
A.H. pitches: G G G E E

Gtrs. I & II B♭5
C5
A.H. (8va)
A.H. (15ma)
Full
P
sl.
A.H. pitches: C C C B♭ G
w/Riff B
Gtr. I G5
1½
2
H P H P
Gtrs. I & II B♭5
A.H. pitch: F
A.H. pitch: G
A.H. pitch: E
A.H. pitches: A♭ G F
A♭ G
w/Riff B
Gtr. I G5
A.H. pitch: F
Gtrs. I & II B♭5
C5
1/2
Full

w/Riff B
Gtr. I G5
8va
Full
trem. pick
1/2
Full
1½
loco
sl.
Gtrs. I & II B♭5
A.H.
(8va)
A.H. pitch: A♭
C5
A.H.
(15ma)
A.H. pitch: B♭
w/Riff B
Gtr. I G5
P.M.
A.H. pitch: D
w/Fill 5
Gtrs. I & II B♭5
A.H. pitch: A♭
A.H. pitch: G
Medium shuffle
Rhy. Fig. 5
G5 E B♭5 E D♭5 C5 B♭5 G5 E B♭5 E D♭5 C5 B♭5 G5
⑥open
1/4
A.H. pitches: E G F F♯ A♭ F
Fdbk.
Fdbk. pitch: D
Fill 5 (Gtr. V)
Fdbk.
(8va)
Fdbk. pitch: F

*Additional Lyrics*

3. Consider me the duke as I dine your dumpster.
Unsanitary engineer.
I'm the bane of the bench, the panhandlin' master.
Well, I'm pullin' twenty G's a year.
Said, I know it ain't much, but at least I'm in touch, yeah,
With reality.
I wouldn't trade no places to be in rat races.
No siree! *(To Chorus)*

# Busy Bee

Words and Music by
Ugly Kid Joe

A
E
yeah.
Ev - 'ry - bod - y's on my mind.
sl.
B
A
(Gtr. I out)
Can't sit a - side and watch this world go by. That ain't me.
Chorus
E
B
A
Aadd9
Bus - y bee watch the world go by.
H
*Gtr. III
let ring throughout
*Electric w/clean tone.

E
B
A
Bus-y bee watch the world_ go by._____ Yeah._____
sl.
2nd Verse
E
w/Fill 1
Now, ev - 'ry-bod - y does their time._____
Fill 1 (Gtr. I)
P
H

A7
E
Those peo-ple walk in crook-ed lines, yeah.
Ev - 'ry-bod - y's got their
B7
A7
choice.
But of-ten, oh, we don't use our voice.

Chorus
E B A E B Aadd9
Bus-y bee watch the world_ go_ by.
sl.
Bus-y bee watch the world__ go by.
E B A
Hmm,
H P

E
B
Aadd9
bus-y bee watch the world_ go by.
(cont. in slashes)
sl.
Bridge
w/Fill 2
Asus2
Gtr. II
Bsus4
Yeah, hmm, bus-y bee watch the world go by.
(World goes
Gtr. III

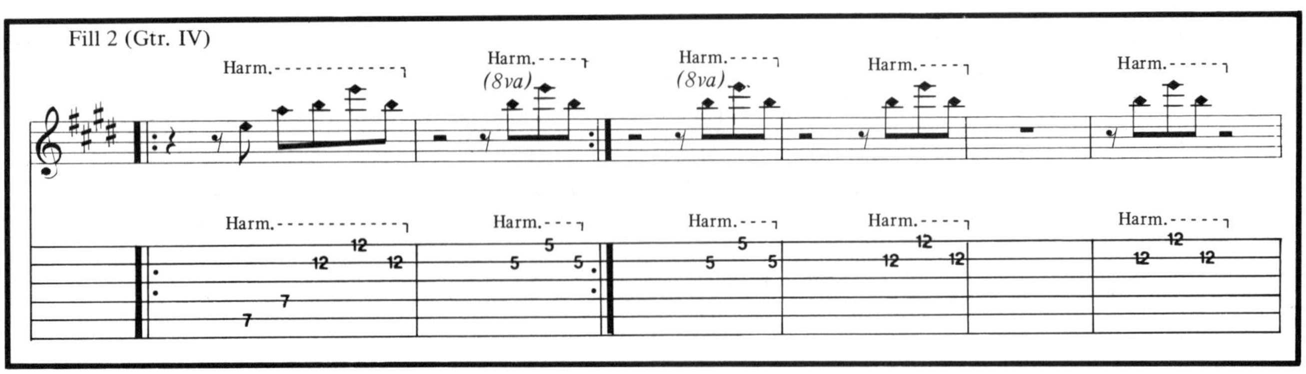
Fill 2 (Gtr. IV)
Harm.
(8va)

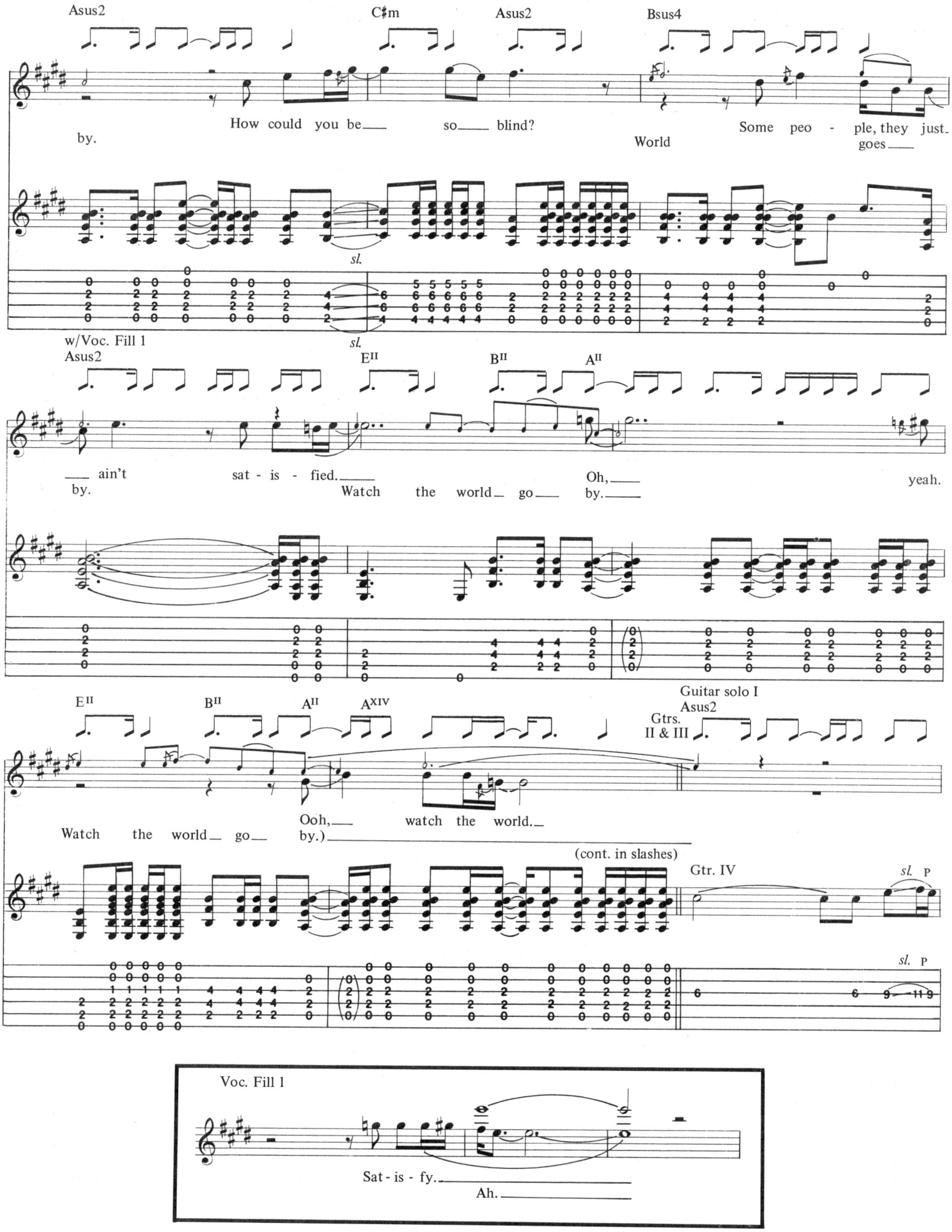
Asus2
C♯m
Asus2
Bsus4
How could you be so blind? Some peo - ple, they just ain't sat - is - fied.
by. World goes by.
sl.
w/Voc. Fill 1
Asus2
EII
BII
AII
Oh, yeah.
Watch the world go by.
EII
BII
AII
AXIV
Guitar solo I
Asus2
Gtrs. II & III
Ooh, watch the world.
Watch the world go by.)
(cont. in slashes)
Gtr. IV
sl. P
Voc. Fill 1
Sat - is - fy.
Ah.

Bsus2
Asus2
C♯m
Asus2
sl.
P
Bsus4
Asus2
E
B5
Asus2
Ooh,
oh.
Gtr. IV
Gtr. V
both notes vib.
Full
*Gtr. IV indicated to left of slashes in TAB.
E^{II}
B5
Asus2
(cont. in notation)
Bus-y bee watch the world go by.
Yeah,
ow.
(Gtrs. IV & V out)

3rd Verse
E
w/Fill 3
I al-ways hear the school bell ring.
Let the chil-dren dance and
Gtr. II
Gtr. III
A7
E
sing, yeah.
Just let us find what's been lost.
Fill 3 (Gtr. I)

Chorus
⑥open
Gtr. III
E EII E B5 Asus2
B A7
So man-y peo - ple get torn and tossed a-way.
(cont. in slashes)
Gtr. IV
sl.
AII Asus2 EII E B5 Asus2
Bus-y bee watch the world go by. Hmm, bus-y bee watch the world go by.

*w/distortion

w/Rhy. Fig. 1 (3 times)
E5
B5
A5
Full
P
H P
P P
P P H
1/2
sl.
E5
B5
A5
E5
B5
A5
Outro
Rhy. Fig. 2
(Gtrs. II & III)
B5
Ooh,
yeah.
(World
goes
A.H.
(15ma)
Full
1½
H
H P
H P P
A.H. pitches: E G G G G G G G E G E
A5
(end Rhy. Fig. 2)
w/Rhy. Fig. 2 (2 times)
B5
A5
Oh, it's go - in' by.
by.
World
goes
by.
Some-times it ain't so great.

w/Rhy. Fig. 1 (3½ times)
B5 A5 E5 B5 A5
It turns, it turns so fast. Ooh.
World goes by. Watch the world go by
HPP
sl.
*Hold note for 2½ bars.
E5 B5 A5
I don't believe, ooh, tell me.
Watch the world go by.
Watch the world, watch the world.
Full
1/2 Full
E5
Gtrs. II & III
E5 B5 A5
Ooh, by.
Watch the world go by.)
Full
Freely
dim.
Ev-'ry-bod-y's al-right with me.
grad. bend
dim.

# Don't Go

Words and Music by
Ugly Kid Joe and Eric Phillips

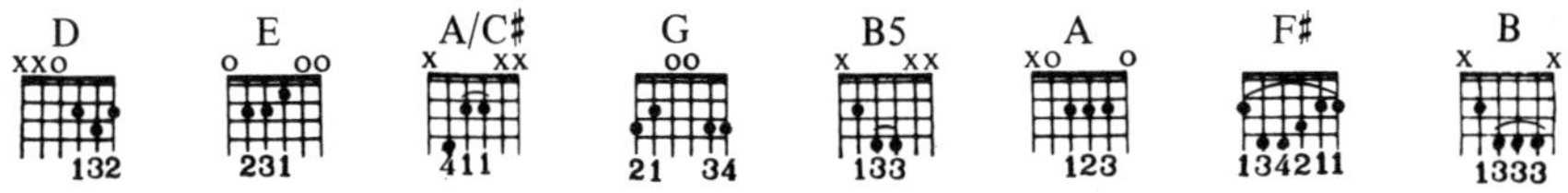


Tune down 1/2 step:
⑥ = E♭ ③ = G♭
⑤ = A♭ ② = B♭
④ = D♭ ① = E♭

**Moderate Rock** ♩ = 108

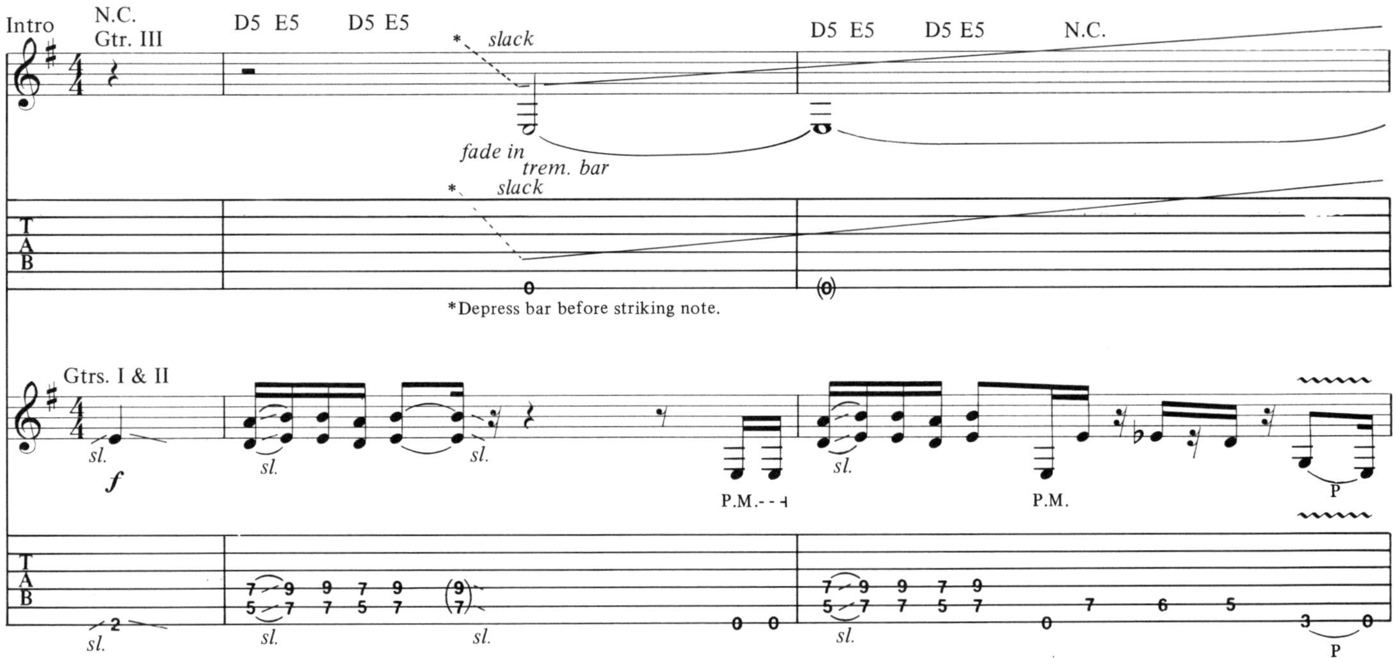


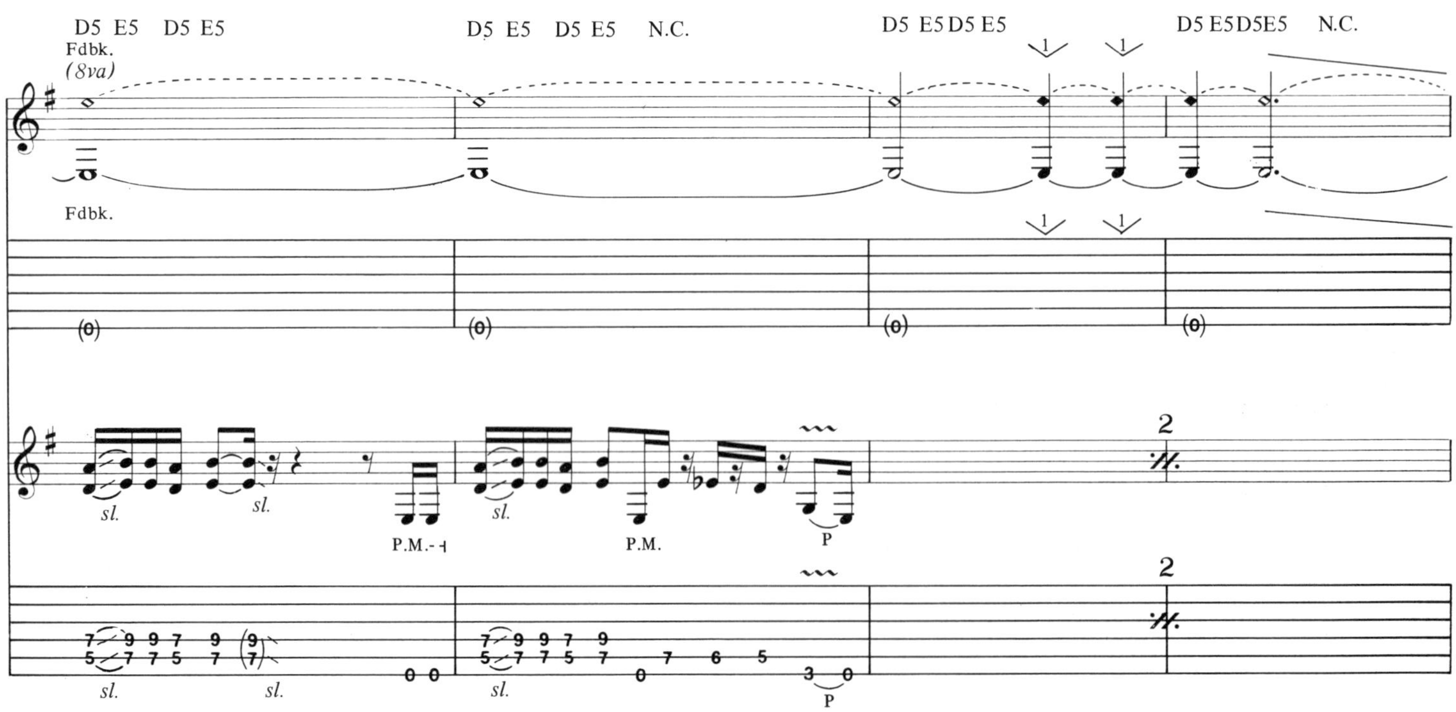

D5 E5 D5 E5
slack 1/2
D5 E5 D5 E5 D5
(Gtr. III out)
sl.
P.M.
E5
D5
A/C♯
D5
This— time, this— time I love you.
Last time, last— time I hate you.
Next— time, ooh,— I need- you.
Gtrs. I & II
E5
D5
Ba - by please- don't go.
A/C♯
D5
A/C
N.C.
3½
trem. bar

1st Verse
D5 E5 D5 E5
D5 A/C♯ D5
E5 D5 E5
Re - mem-ber when I met you,
school_ dress
Rhy. Fig. 1 (Gtrs. I & II)
sl.
P.M.
D5 A5 N.C.
D5 E5 D5 E5
D5 A/C♯ D5
on.___
I nev - er could for - get you,
Gtr. I substitute Rhy. Fill 1
D5 E5 D5 E5
D5 A5 B♭5
and ba - by, now you're gone.___
(end Rhy. Fig. 1)
Rhy. Fill 1 (Gtr. I)
A.H.
(8va)
A.H. pitch: A♭

Pre-chorus
B5
w/Fill 1
D5/A
I'm go - in' 'round and 'round to - day, just try'n' to find the truth.
Rhy. Fig. 2 (Gtr. I)
H P.M. P P.M.
H P.M. H P.M. P.M.
Rhy. Fig. 2A (Gtr. II)
H P.M. P.M. P.M.
H P.M. H P.M. P.M.
Rhy. Fill 2
(Gtr. IV - acous.)
D
B5
Does-n't real - ly mat - ter an - y - way when I'm liv - ing with - out you.
(end Rhy. Fig. 2)
(end Rhy. Fig. 2A)
Fill 1
Full
grad. bend

Chorus
Rhy. Fig. 3A (Gtr. IV acous.)
E D A/C# D G
This_ time, this_ time I love you.
Last_ time, aw, last_ time I hate you.
Next_ time, ooh,_ I need_ you.
Rhy. Fig. 3 (Gtrs. I & II)
P
E
Ba - by please_ don't go._
(end Rhy. Fig. 3A) (Gtr. IV out)
(end Rhy. Fig. 3)
P.M.
sl.
2nd Verse
w/Rhy. Fig. 1
D5E5 D5 E5
I said come on lit - tle dar - lin'.
D5 A/C# D5
D5 E5 D5 E5
Ba - by don't you_ see._
D5 A5 N.C.
D5 E5 D5 E5
I'd nev - er do you harm - in',_
w/Fill 2
D5 A/C# D5
no._
D5 E5 D5 E5
Just you and me,_
Gtr. I substitute Rhy. Fill 1
D5 A5 B♭5
yeah.
Pre-chorus
w/Rhy. Figs. 2 & 2A (both 1st 3 bars only)
B5
I'm on the cor - ner right_ now,_
w/Fill 1
wait - in' for_ your love._
D5/A B5
You bet - ter make a choice_ now_ be - fore a
Fill 2
A.H. (8va)
A.H. A.H. (8va)(8va)
H
A.H. pitch: B

w/Rhy. Fill 3 (Gtrs. I & II) N.C.
w/Rhy. Figs. 2 & 2A
B5
w/Fill 1
D5/A
push comes to a shove.
Yeah, things seem kind-a dif-f'rent, it ain't the way it was.
B5
w/Rhy. Fill 2
D5
Re-mem-ber what your ma-ma said; the bond that lies is us.
Chorus
w/Rhy. Figs. 3 & 3A (both 2 times)
E
D
A/C♯
D
G
This time, this time I love you.
Last time, aw, last time I hate you.
Next time, ooh, I need you.
1.
Substitute Rhy. Fill 4 (Gtrs. I, II & IV)
E
Ba-by please don't go.
2.
E
Ba-by please don't go. Good God!
Interlude
N.C.(E5)
Gtrs. I & II
1.2.3.
4.
(cont. in slashes)
H
P.M.
P P
sl.
Gtrs. I & II
B5
Gtr. III
P.M.
sl.
Full
pick slides
pick slide
Rhy. Fill 3 (Gtrs. I & II)
H
P.M.
P
Rhy. Fill 4
E
Gtr. IV
Gtrs. I & II

Guitar solo
D5 E5 D5 E5
Full
P
D5
A/C♯
D5
E5
D5
E5
w/harmonizer
D5
A5
N.C.
D5 E5 D5 E5
sl.
A/C♯
1/2
E5
D5
E5
Gtr. I substitute Rhy. Fill 2
D5
A5
B♭5
(cont. in Fill 3)
w/Rhy. Figs. 2 & 2A (both 1st 3 bars only) and Fill 3
B5
Gtr. V
H
D5/A
B5
Fill 3 (Gtr. III)

Full
A.H.
Full
trem. bar
slack
A.H.
(8va)
C5 C♯5 D5 D♯5 E5
(Gtr. V out)
trem. bar
A.H. pitch: A
Gtrs. I & II
P.M.
sl.
*Gtr. II only.
Rhy. Fig. 4 (Gtr. IV acous.)
3rd Verse
E
D
A
I'm by the phone, and I'm all a - lone, just a - wait - in' and a - pray - in' that may - be you'll
Gtr. IV (clean elec.)
let ring
Gtr. VII (clean elec.)
let ring

E
w/Rhy. Fig. 4
E
D
call.
I got-ta know right now should I stay a-round, should I stay a-while, should I
A
Gtrs. I & II E
(cont. in notation)
Rhy. Fig. 5 (Gtr. IV acous.)
F♯
stand here cry'n' or ba-by should I fly?
Yeah, yeah!
Ooh, come on dar-lin', don't you
Rhy. Fig. 5A (Gtr. VI)
(Gtr. VII out)
Rhy. Fig. 5B (Gtrs. I & II)

(end Rhy. Fig. 5)
see and don't you know?
I got-ta have your lov-in', ba-by, now now, I'll nev-er let ya go.
(end Rhy. Fig. 5A)
(end Rhy. Fig. 5B)
w/Rhy. Figs. 5, 5A & 5B
I'm look-in' round and round, try'n' to find that girl of mine. She's so far a-way and I am
Chorus
w/Rhy. Figs. 5, 5A & 5B (all 2½ times)
cry-in', yeah! Ba-by.
Woh, ba-ba-by yeah, yeah.
This time. Last time.
8va
Gtr. III
Full
Where ya go-in', where are you right now, oh?
Next time.
H P

E
B
E
A
Say, say, say it yeah. Well, I need ya so. Nev-er ev-er nev-er gon-na ev-er let ya go,
This time. Last time. Next time.
loco
1½
Full
1/2
P
F♯
yeah ba-by. No, no, no. No, no, no.
This time. Last time.
w/Fill 4
Gtr. IV
rit.
Gtrs. I & VI
Freely
dim.
Gtr. II
H
*Pitch raised and lowered w/tuning peg.
Fill 4 (Gtr. III)

# So Damn Cool

Words and Music by
Ugly Kid Joe

1st, 2nd Verses
w/Rhy. Fig. 1 (Gtrs. I & II)
N.C.(D5)
1. I wan - na know why the peo - ple are ev - 'ry - where. And
2. See additional lyrics.
I wan - na know where to go if I get scared. And
I wan - na be in a place where no one cares. And
A G sl.
I wan - na know you be - cause you're so damn
(Ah.)
w/Rhy. Figs. 1 & 2 (Both 2 times)
N.C.(D5)
1.
cool. Yeah, you're so damn cool.
2.
w/Rhy. Figs. 1 & 2 (Both 2 times)
cool. You're just so damn cool. Yeah, you're so damn cool.
Rhy. Fig. 3 (Two gtrs.)
Bridge
A5 G5 D/F♯ G5
Who knows what I'm feel - in' in - side
A5 AXII A5 G5 D A5 sl.
of me. Who knows if I'm feel - in' al - right.
AXII A5 G5 D/F♯ G5 A5 AXII sl.
Who knows what I'm feel - in' in - side of me.
(end Rhy. Fig. 3)
A5 G5 D A5 AXII sl.
Who knows what is run - nin' a - round in my brain.

Gtr. w/Rhy. Fig. 2 (2 times)
N.C.(D5)
*w/Telephone-conversation voices (till double bar).
w/Fill 1
Gtr. I
A5
*Gtr. II
G5
* Standard tuning (tuned down a half step).
D/F♯
P.M.
A.H.
(15ma)
Full
sl.
A.H. pitch: F♯
8va
Fill 1 (Gtr. II)
Harm.
(8va)

D
A5
8va
sl.
A5
G5
D/F♯
G5
A5
Who
knows.
Full
(Gtr. II out)
Gtr. III
A.H. (15ma)
A.H. pitch: F♯
A5
G5
w/Rhy. Fig. 2 (3 times)
N.C.(D5)
Who
knows.
w/wah
sl.

8va
w/delay
15 12 14 12 13 13 16 13 15 13 14 14 17 14 16 16 15 15 18 15 17 15 14 14
17 14 16 14 15 15 18 15 17 15 16 16 19 16 18 16 17 17 20 17 19 17 16 16
w/Rhy. Fig. 1 (1st bar only)
Oh.
Full
slow bend
19 16 18 16 17 17 20 17 19 17 18 18 21 18 20 18 19 19 22 19 21 19 19 19
22
w/Rhy. Fig. 3
A5
G5
D/F♯
Now that I'm done and I seen it, and don't think that I'm try - in' to
(Who knows what I'm feel - in' in - side
(Gtr. III out)
(22)
A5
A<sup>XII</sup>
com - plain.
of me.
Don't think I'm ly'n' 'cause I feel it. And all you
Who knows
D
peo - ple out there don't look at me too late. All your blame 'cause you need
feel - in' al - right.
Who
knows.

*Additional Lyrics*

2. I wanna feel like I'm floating in the air.  
And I wanna know if the sun's gonna bleach my hair.  
And I wanna know why life's just so unfair.  
And I wanna know you because you're so damn cool.  
Yeah, you're so damn cool. You're just so damn cool.  
Yeah, you're so damn cool. *(To Bridge)*

# Same Side

Words and Music by
Ugly Kid Joe

1st Verse
w/Riff A
Rhy. Fig. 1A
A5
(Gtr. II)
sl.
(Gtr. II out)
N.C.(D7/F♯)
(Am7)
does - n't mat - ter who you are, or what you're gon - na be.
Peo - ple from all walks of life, you got - ta
(D7/F♯)
(Am7)
(D7/F♯)
Dsus4
have di - ver - si - ty.
We're all in this to - geth - er, and to - geth - er we shall be.
You got - ta
1/2
H
P
Am11
N.C.(D7/F♯)
be a friend - ly neigh - bor, if you're gon - na live next to me.
We're all
Full
Riff A (Gtr. III)

Chorus
w/Rhy. Fig. 1
A5 G5 A5 C5 A5 G5 F♯5 C5 D5 C5 A5 G5 A5 G5 A5 C5 A5 G5
liv - in' on the same side,_ same side of town._ Walk - in' down the same streets,_ the
F♯5 G5 ⑥ open E 2fr. F♯ 3fr. G C5
streets that are all a - round._
2nd Verse
w/Rhy. Fig. 1A & Riff A
A5 N.C.(D7/F♯)
Now, you could by my broth - er, or you could be my friend._ But,
(Am7) (D7/F♯) (Am7)
don't you turn your back on me,_'cause we'll be here 'til the end._ We're all in this to-geth - er,_ and we
(D7/F♯) (Am7) (D7/F♯) Dsus4
all have_ that dream._ To live in per - fect har - mo - ny,_ like a fam - i - ly, that's the scene._'Cause, we're all

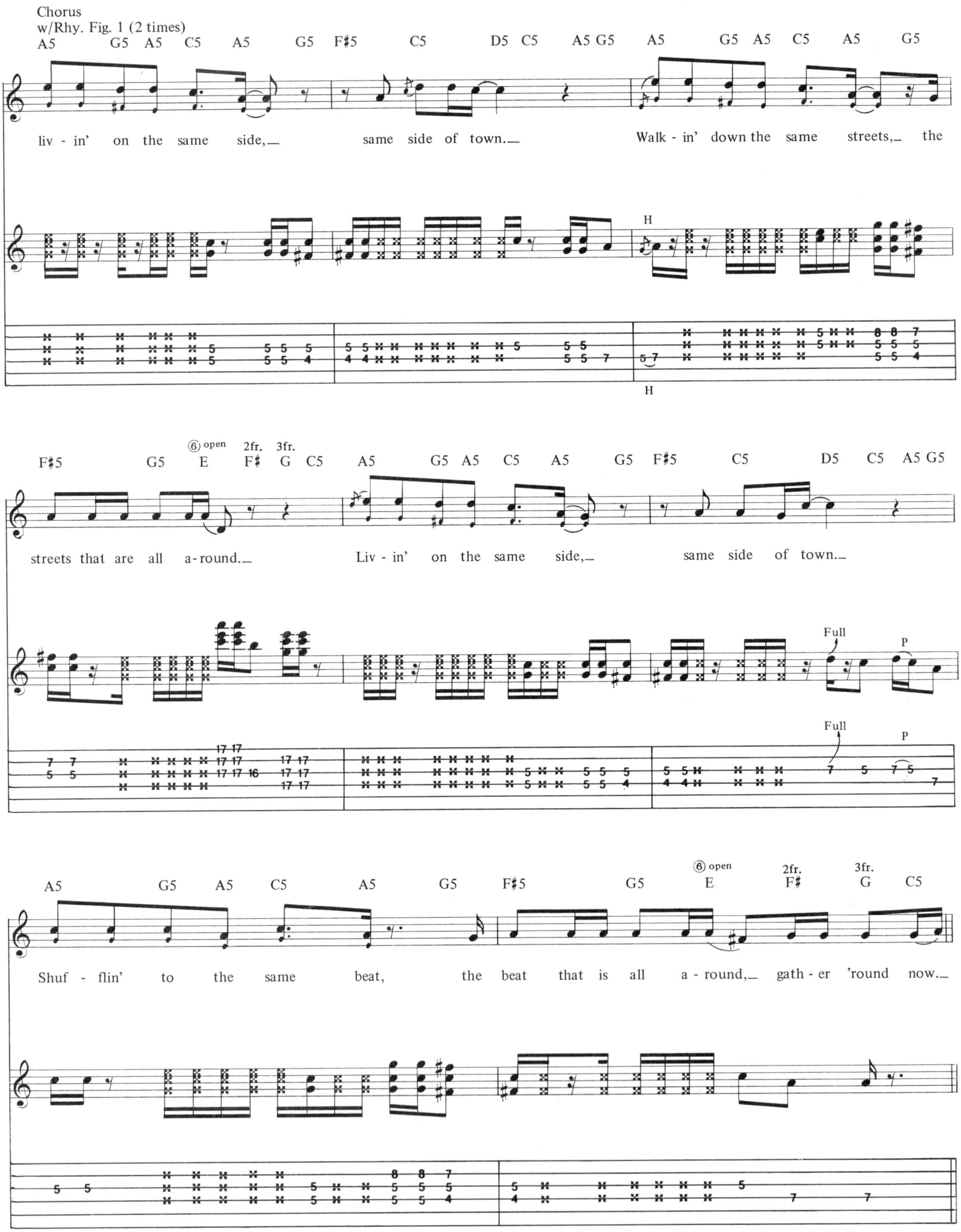
Chorus
w/Rhy. Fig. 1 (2 times)
A5 G5 A5 C5 A5 G5 F♯5 C5 D5 C5 A5 G5 A5 G5 A5 C5 A5 G5
liv - in' on the same side, same side of town. Walk - in' down the same streets, the
H
H
F♯5 G5 ⑥ open E 2fr. F♯ 3fr. G C5 A5 G5 A5 C5 A5 G5 F♯5 C5 D5 C5 A5 G5
streets that are all a-round. Liv - in' on the same side, same side of town.
Full
P
A5 G5 A5 C5 A5 G5 F♯5 G5 ⑥ open E 2fr. F♯ 3fr. G C5
Shuf - flin' to the same beat, the beat that is all a - round, gath - er 'round now.

w/Rhy. Fig. 1A
A5
Gtr. III
Am11
*Vol. knob swell.
Gtr. I
w/echo repeats
sl.
P
1/4
Full
H P H
H
w/vocal sound effects
don't pick

N.C.(Am)
(D)
(Am)
Ah ah ah.
Ba, ba, ba, da, ba.
Ah ah ah, ba ba da da ba,
1.
(D)
ba ba da da ba ba.
2.
(D)
ba ba da da ba ba.
Get to it.

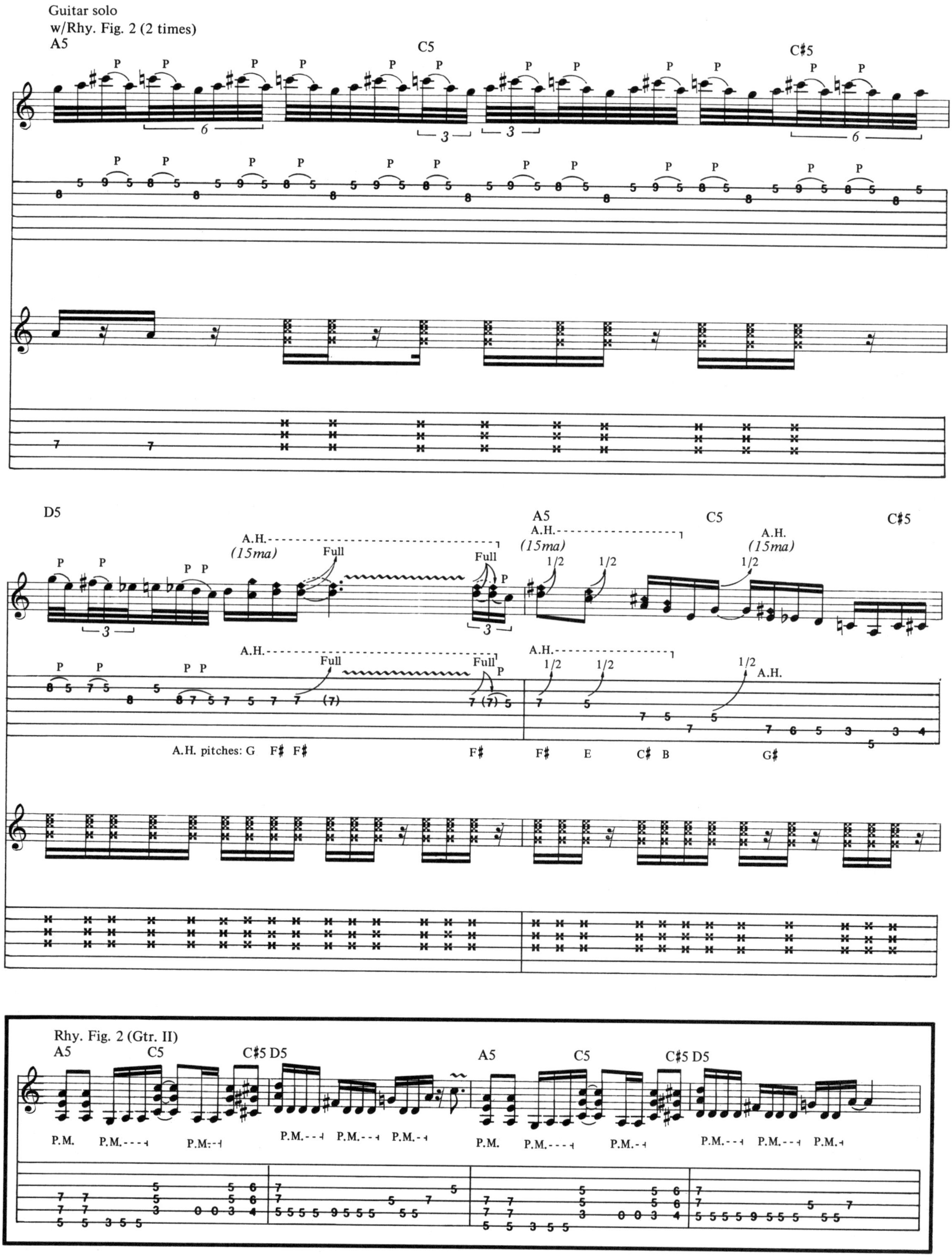
Guitar solo
w/Rhy. Fig. 2 (2 times)
A5
C5
C♯5
D5
A.H.
(15ma)
Full
1/2
A.H. pitches: G F♯ F♯
F♯
F♯ E C♯ B G♯
Rhy. Fig. 2 (Gtr. II)
C♯5 D5
P.M.

D5
A5
C5
C♯5
D5
8va
Full
sl.
don't pick
P
H
sl. loco
A.H.
(15ma)
2½
A.H. pitch: G♯
pick slide
Fdbk.
w/Rhy. Fig. 2
1/2

A5
C5
C♯5
D5
8va
Full
1½
(Gtr. III out)
sl.
don't pick
straight 16's
3rd Verse
w/Riff A
N.C.(Am7)
(D7/F♯)
(Am7)
Stum-blin' down on D. P., keg-gers all a-round. Laugh-in' at the po-lice as they
Gtr. I
(D7/F♯)
(Am7)
(D7/F♯)
try to bring us down. We're hang-in' with each oth-er, yes we're hang-in' with our bro's. We
(Am7)
(D7/F♯)
Dsus4
Chorus
w/Rhy. Fig. 1 (2 times)
A5 G5 A5 C5 A5 G5
all love one an-oth-er, from our heads down to our toes. 'Cause we're all liv-in' on the same side,

F♯5 C5 D5 C5 A5 G5 A5 G5 A5 C5 A5 G5 F♯5 G5 E F♯ G C5
⑥open 2fr. 3fr.
same side of town.
Walk - in' down the same streets, the streets that are all a - round. Liv -
H
A5 G5 A5 C5 A5 G5 F♯5 C5 D5 C5 A5 G5 A5 G5 A5 C5 A5 G5
in' on the same side, same side of town.
Shuf - flin' to the same beat, the
P
sl.
F♯5 G5 E F♯ G5 C5
beat that is all a - round. Yeah, come on.
Outro
w/Rhy. Fig. 2 (3 times)
A5 C5 C♯5 D5
Get to it.
(Liv - in' on the same side.
Oh, yeah.
Gtr. III
Full
trem. pick
Gtr. I

A5 C5 C♯5 D5 A5 C5 C♯5
Liv - in' on the same_ side.
Think a - bout it.
Liv - in' on the same side.
D5 A5 C5 C♯5
Oh, yeah._
Liv - in' on the same_ side,

w/lead vocal ad lib. (next 8 bars)
D5
A5
C5
C♯5
same side of town.)
8va
loco
sl.
Full
1/4
A.H.
(15ma)
P.M.
A.H. pitch: G
w/Rhy. Fig. 2 (1st 3 bars only)
A5
C5
C♯5
D5
1/2

w/Rhy. Fill 1
N.C.
(Am)
(D)
Full
P
sl.
Gtr. IV
Gtr. III
1/2
Rhy. Fill 1 (Gtr. II)
(Gtr. II out)

# Cat's In The Cradle

Words and Music by
Harry Chapin and Sandy Chapin

All gtrs.
tune down ½ step:
⑥ = E♭ ③ = G♭
⑤ = A♭ ② = B♭
④ = D♭ ① = E♭

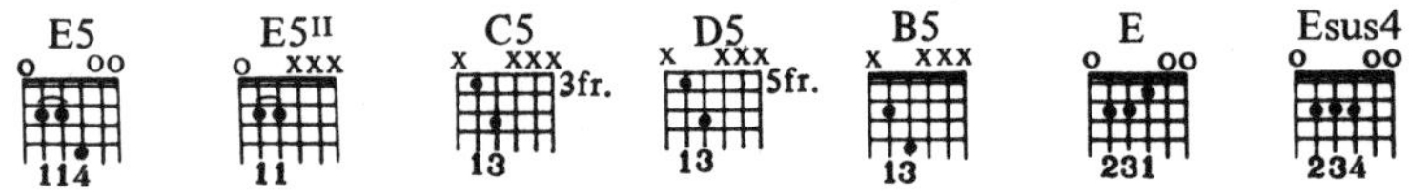


**Moderately** 𝅗𝅥 = 78

*Six stg. elec. capoed at 7fr. TAB numbers indicate actual fret numbers; 7fr. is thought of as an open stg.

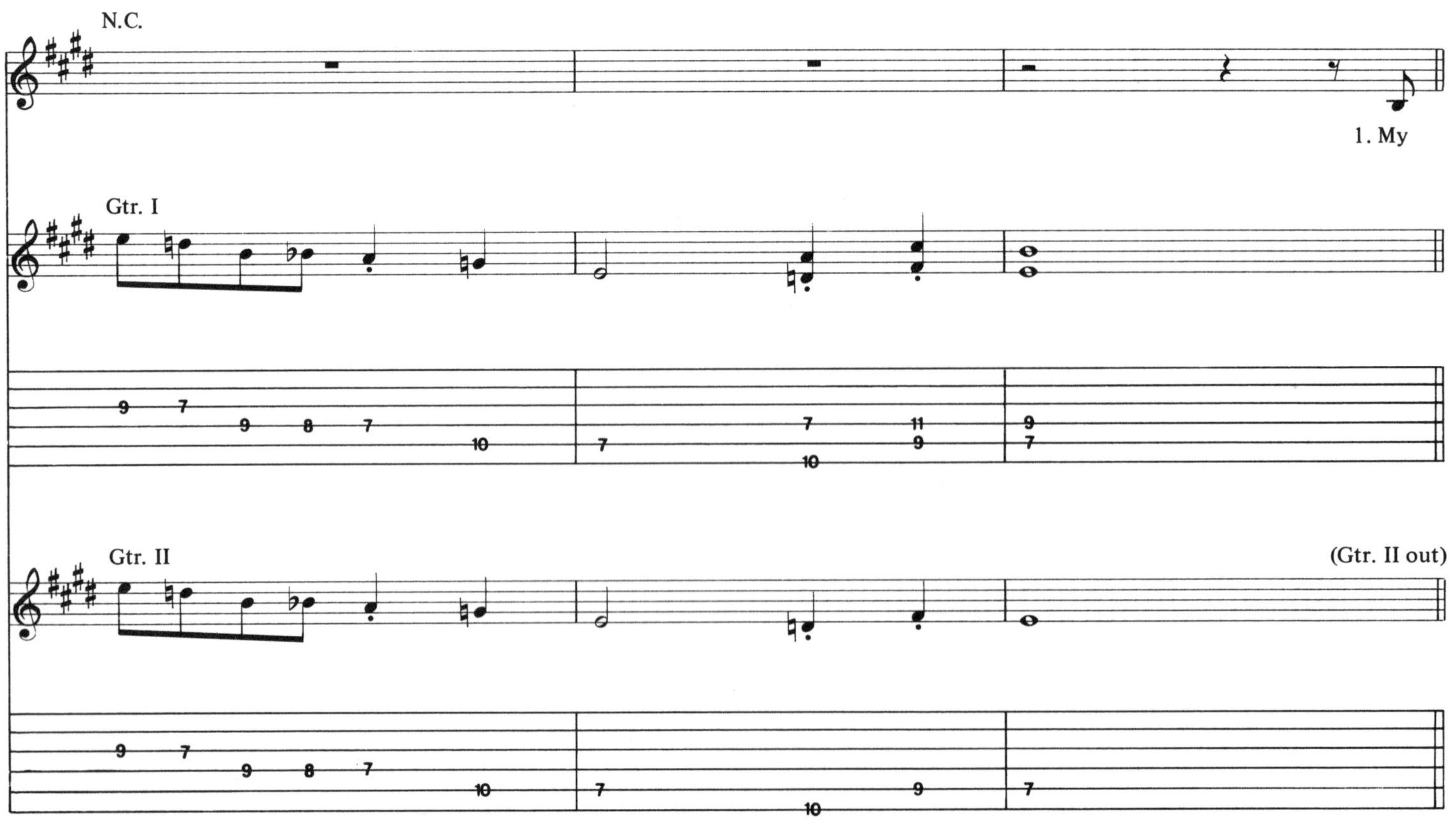

*Chorus voc. doubled an octave lower.

Chorus
E5
D
Dsus4
D
G5
cat's in the cra-dle and the sil-ver spoon,
lit-tle boy blue and the man
Rhy. Fig. 3 (Gtr. I)
mf
A
Asus4
A
E5
D
Dsus4
D
'n the moon.
1.2. "When you com-in' home?" "Son, I don't know when.
3. "When you com-in' home, Son?" "I don't know when.
Gsus2
D/F♯
E
Gsus2
D/F♯
To Coda
E5
We'll get to-geth-er then.
You know we'll have a good time then."
H
w/Riff A
E5
Gtr. I
1.
2.
D.S. al Coda
2. Well, my
3. Well, he

Coda
Gtr. III (elec.)
E5II
C5
D5
B5
then,
yeah."
Gtr. I
E5II
w/Fill 1
C5
D5
B5
E5II
dim.
I've

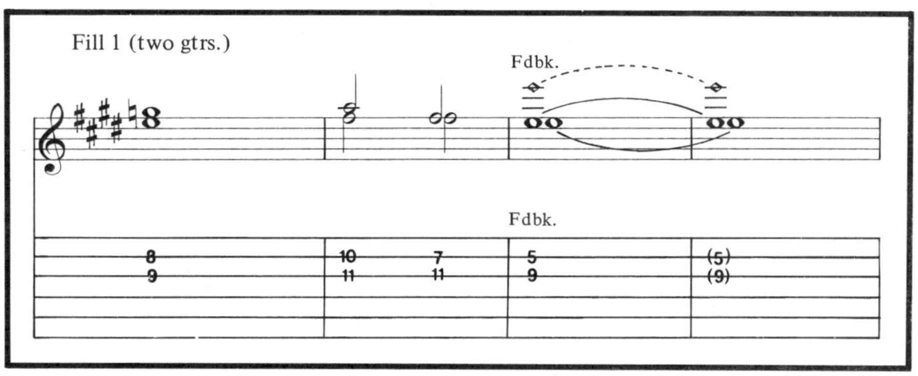
Fill 1 (two gtrs.)
Fdbk.
Fdbk.

*Chorus vocal is tripled (sung one octave higher and one octave lower).

*Additional Lyrics*

2. Well, my son turned ten just the other day.
He said, "Thanks for the ball, Dad. Come on, let's play.
Could you teach me to throw? " I said, "Not today.
I got a lot to do." He said, "That's okay."
And he walked away and he smiled and he said, "You know,
I'm gonna be like him, yeah.
You know I'm gonna be like him." *(To Chorus)*

3. Well, he came from college just the other day,
So much like a man I just had to say,
"I'm proud of you. Could you sit for a while?"
He shook his head and he said with a smile,
"What I'd really like, Dad, is to borrow the car keys.
See you later. Can I have them please?" *(To Chorus)*

# I'll Keep Tryin'

Words and Music by
Ugly Kid Joe and Alan Reed

Tune down ½ step:
⑥ = E♭ ③ = G♭
⑤ = A♭ ② = B♭
④ = D♭ ① = E♭

1st, 2nd Verses
E5
1. If I had the time and lots - a mon - ey, then I'd take you 'round the world. 'N'
if I was the king and had a cas - tle, then you'd sure - ly be my queen. 'N'
if I had a dime for ev - 'ry pen - ny, then I'd buy you dia - monds, girl.
we would live up in the tall - est tow - er and we rare - ly would be seen.
G5
You don't e - ven know how much I love you and how much I wan - na be your
You don't e - ven know how much I need you and how much you mean to me. I'm a
E5
knight in shin - in' ar - mor. Yeah, ba - by, that's good e - nough for me. And I'll keep
dog with - out a bone. You hear me cry - in' and it's time for you to see that I'll keep
P.M.
sl.
semi-harm.
*P.M. 1st time only.
H P P
*Play one notes 2nd time.

Chorus
A5
try - in', yeah, I'll keep try - in' to make you
Rhy. Fig. 1
1/4
sl.
E7
mine, ooh, mine all mine. I hope you're
P.M. P.M.
P
A5
buy - in', I hope you're buy - in' all of my
(end Rhy. Fig. 1)
N.C.
1.
lines. Ooh. Ah. 2. Now

2.
(end half time feel)
Guitar solo
E5
Gtr. II
sl.
mf
P.M.
w/Fill 1
P H P H P H P H P
Fill 1
8va
Gtr. III
Full

A5
sl.
slack
Full
trem. bar (slow dive)
P.M.
H P
A.H.
(15ma)
semi-harm.
A.H. pitches: G F♯ A G A G
E7
1/2
P

B5
Full
slack
trem. bar (slow dive)
1½
grad. bend 1½
P
A5
P H P
1/2
sl.
N.C.
A.H.
(15ma)
1/4

(Gtr. II out)
E5
sl.
steady gliss.
sl.
w/Riff A (4 times)
E5
Ooh.
Ooh.
*w/Riff B (4 times)
N.C.
Oh.
Oh.
*Grad. cresc. from mp to f
Riff A
Gtr. I
mp
P.M.
sl.
sl.
Riff B
Gtr. I

Just stay.
Just stay.
Half time feel
Chorus
w/Rhy. Fig. 1
A5
And I'll keep try - in', yeah, I'll keep try - in'
E7
to make you mine.
Ooh, talk to me.
A5
I hope you're buy - in', I hope you're buy - in'
N.C.
all of my, my, my, my, my, my,
(Gtr. I)
1/4
my, my, my, my, my, my, my, my, my,
N.C.
lines!
(Sing 1st time only)
*Riff C
P.M.
*Play non-P.M. notes with random artificial harmonics.

w/Riff C (6 times)
N.C.
Gtr. II
P.M.
(Gtr. II out)
sl.
4
w/Riff D (till end)
N.C.
Gtr. I
Repeat and fade
Riff D
Gtr. II
mp

# Everything About You

Words and Music by
Ugly Kid Joe

All gtrs. tune down 1/2 step:
(6) = E♭ (3) = G♭
(5) = A♭ (2) = B♭
(4) = D♭ (1) = E♭

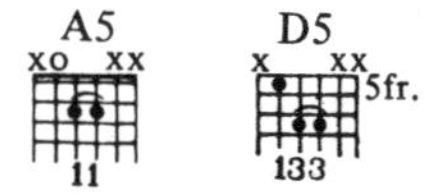

1st, 2nd Verses
D5
A5
D
A5
1. I
hate the rain and sun-ny weath - er.
And
2. See additional lyrics
P.M.
P.M.
let ring
I,
I hate the beach and moun-tains too,
boo hoo.
P
I
don't like a thing a - bout the cit - y,
no, no.
Gtr. II
Gtr. I

D5 A5 D5 A5 1.
I, I, I hate the coun-try-side too. And
P.M. P.M.
1/2
G5 A5 D5 A5
I hate ev-'ry-thing a-bout you. Ev-'ry-thing a-bout
Gtrs. I & II
let ring
D5 A5 N.C. 2.
you. And And
Gtr. II
Gtr. I
sl.
P.M.

Chorus
G5
A5
G5
A5
I get sick when I'm a - round, I can't stand to be a - round,
Rhy. Fig. 2
(Gtrs. I & II)
let ring
let ring
G5
A5
D5
A5
I hate ev - 'ry - thing a - bout you. Ev - 'ry - thing a - bout
(end Rhy. Fig. 2)
sl.
let ring
P.M.
P.M.
D5
A5
D5
A5
you. Hate ev - 'ry - thing a - bout you. Ev - 'ry - thing a - bout
P.M.
P.M.
P
P.M.
P.M.
D5
C5
A5
Half time feel
Bridge
G5
you. Some say I got a bad at - ti - tude,
let ring
(clean tone)

A5
G5
but that don't change the way I feel a - bout you.
And if you think this might be
bring - in' me down,
A5
look a - gain 'cause I ain't wear - in' no frown. Get down!
*P.M.
*distortion on
sl.
Guitar solo
w/Rhy. Fig. 1
D5
A5
D5
A5
8va
Gtr. III
Full
w/Rhy. Fig. 1 (1st 2 bars only - 2 times)
D5
A5
D5
A5
1/2
Full Full

w/Rhy. Fig. 2
G5 A5 G5 A5
8va
loco
sl.
trem. bar
G5 A5 D5
Gtrs. I & II
p f
Full
let ring
(Gtr. III out)
*Tap w/edge of pick.
Double time feel
D5 A7 A7
1.2.3.
4.
Rhy. Fig. 3
(Gtrs. I & II)
(Spoken:) Well,
3rd Verse
w/Rhy. Fig. 3 (6 times)
D7 A7
I don't real-ly care a-bout your sis-ter, for-get the lit-tle bitch 'cause I al-read-y kissed her.
One thing that I did to your old la-dy, put her on the bed and she did-n't say may-be.
I know, you know, ev-'ry-bod-y knows, the way it comes, the way it's gon-na go. You
think it's sad, well that's too bad, 'cause I'm hav-in' a ball hat-in' ev-'ry lit-tle thing a-bout

*Additional Lyrics*

2. And I don't like a thing about your mother.
   And I, I hate your daddy's guts too, boo hoo.
   And I don't like a thing about your sister, no, no.
   'Cause I, I, I think sex is overrated too. *(To Chorus)*

# Madman ('92 Re-Mix)

Words and Music by
Ugly Kid Joe

Tune down 1/2 step:
⑥ = E♭ ③ = G♭
⑤ = A♭ ② = B♭
④ = D♭ ① = E♭

N.C.(A5)
D5 C5 D5 C5
Hand in hand, to Dis - ney - land we go! (w/echo repeats) Not
P.M.
tr
slow. Ah,
(1st,) 2nd Verses
N.C.(A5)
(1.) hap - pi - est place in the world
here, lit - tle girl, if you wan - na see Pet - er
sl.
'til a mad - man grabs a girl. Hand in hand
Pan's Mag-ic Flight on L. S. D. Up and down,
with the mad - man she
all a - round they
H
goes! (w/echo repeats) Woh oh.
go! (w/echo repeats) Woh oh.
Chorus
E5
Eb5
Knife gleam - in',
semi-harm.

D5 D♯5 E5 D5 C5 D5
no feel - in's, axe wield - in', child steal - in', mad - man's loose in Dis - ney -
P.M. sl.
1.
N.C.(A5)
land.
P.M. P.M. P.M. sl.
(E5)
2. Come land.
2.
N.C.(A5)
In Dis - ney -
land.
(E5)
D5 C5 D5 C5
Mad - man is loose in

D5 C5 A5 D5 C5 D5 C5 D5 C5 A5
Dis - ney - land. He's back here by pop - u - lar de - mand.
sl.
D5 C5 D5 C5 D5 C5 A5 D5 C5 D5 C5
Mad - man is loose in Dis - ney - land. He'll take no lip, but he'll
sl.
D5 C5 A5
take your head!
trem. bar
A5 G5 A5 G5 D5 A5 G5
pick slide
sl.
P.M.

3rd Verse
A5 D5 C5 A5 G5 A5 G5 D5
Sur - prise, sur - prise. I'm com - in' at ya live.
A.H. (15ma)
P.M. A.H.
A.H. pitch: G
A5 G5 A5 D5 C5 D5 C5
Sure as hell ain't Mick - ey Mouse, I'm a kill - er in dis - guise. You could run, and
D5 C5 F5 A5 G5 A5 D5 C5
you could hide, but you ain't get - tin' a - way 'cause I got you in my sight. Axe
Chorus
E5 Eb5 D5 D♯5 E5 D5
wield - in', child steal - in', I'm a mad moth - er and I'm loose in Dis - ney -
pick slide
sl.

Guitar solo
w/Fill 1
N.C.(A5)
(D5)
(A5)
land.
Gtr. I
8va
w/delay
grad. bend
Full
P
Gtr. II
P.M.
tr
(E5)
1/2
loco

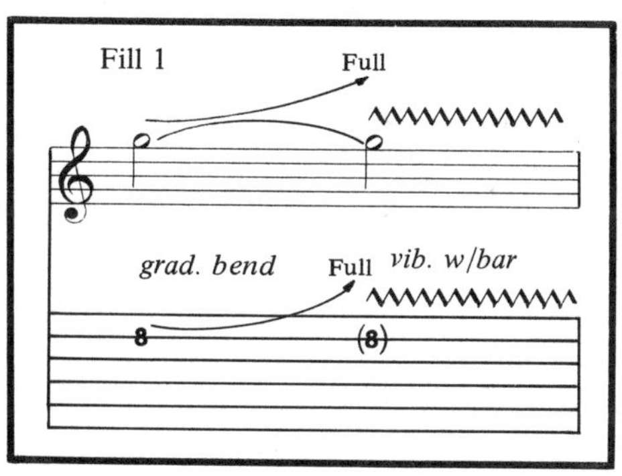
Fill 1
Full
grad. bend
vib. w/bar

*Gtr. II w/flanger (next 8 bars).

(A5)
(D5)
Have his— way— with you. Noth - in'— you— can do. Head - lines— in— the news.
P.M.
E5
N.C.(A5)
Mad - man— sure— is loose. Dis - ney - land.
Gtr. I
sl.
tr
Both gtrs.
E
Gtr. I
Gtr. II
Both gtrs.
4th Verse
N.C.(A5)
Dis - ney - land's— the place— to be, in Cal - i - for - nia, by— the sea.
H

D5 C5 D5 C5 D5 C5 D5 C5 N.C.(A5)
Sun - ny day, we're A - O. K. for now, and
P.M. P.M. P.M.
Chorus
E5 Eb5 D5 D#5
how. Knife gleam - in', no feel - in's, axe
P.M. P.M. P.M. sl.
E D C5 D5 N.C.(A5)
wield - in', child steal - in', mad - man's lost in Dis - ney - land.
semi-harm.
P.M. sl.
In Dis - ney - land, oh.
P.M. P.M. sl.
semi-harm.

# Mr. Recordman

Words and Music by
Ugly Kid Joe

Half time feel
1st, 2nd Verses
G C D C G/B N.C.
1. I've tak - en a lik - in' to your game.
2. Don't need much time to think a - bout.
Rhy. Fig. 2
(end Rhy. Fig. 2)
let ring let ring H
H
w/Rhy. Fig. 2 (3 times)
G C D
w/Fill 1
C G/B N.C.
I think we all, we feel the same.
I'm sure that you have got the clout.
G C D C G/B N.C.
Is this a dream or is it real?
I on - ly hope that you're my friend,
G C D
w/Fill 1
(end half time feel)
C G/B N.C.
You say you want to cut a deal.
and stand by me un - til the end.
Mis - ter
Chorus
w/Rhy. Fig. 1 (4 times)
w/Fill 2
G Cadd9 G D G Cadd9 G D
Rec - ord - man, do you know who I am? Mis - ter
w/Fill 2
G Cadd9 G D G Cadd9 G D
Rec - ord - man, do you real - ly think I can?
Fill 1 (Gtr. II)
Fill 2 (Gtr. II)
8va

w/Rhy. Fig. 1 (4 times)
w/Fill 2
G Cadd9 G D G Cadd9 G D
Sell a lot-ta rec-ords 'n' tour 'round the world. Make a lot-ta mon-ey 'n' meet lots-a girls. Mis-ter
w/Fill 2
G Cadd9 G D G Cadd9 G D
Rec-ord - man, do you real-ly think I can?
(Mis-ter Rec-ord - man.)
Guitar solo
w/Rhy. Fig. 1 (8 times)
Gtr. II
1/2
Full
sl.
P
8va
loco

G Cadd9 G D G Cadd9 G
8va
Full Full
P P P P
H
D G
sl.
Half time feel
3rd Verse
w/Rhy. Fig. 2 (2 times)
G C D
It sounds like mu - sic to my ears.
C G/B N.C. G C
I've dreamed of this for man - y years.
w/Fill 1
(end half time feel) w/Rhy. Fig. 1 (4 times)
D C G/B N.C. G Cadd9 G
To sell a lot - ta rec - ords 'n' tour
w/Fill 2
D G Cadd9 G D
'round the world. Make a lot - ta mon - ey 'n' meet lots - a girls.
w/Fill 2
G Cadd9 G D G Cadd9 G
Have a lot of fun and hang with my bro's, 'cause these boys 'n' this band is
Chorus
w/Rhy. Fig. 1 (4 times)
w/Fill 2
D G Cadd9 G D
all I know. Mis - ter Rec - ord - man, do you
(Mis - ter Rec - ord - man.)

G Cadd9 G D G Cadd9 G
know who I am? Mis - ter Rec - ord - man,
(Mis - ter
w/Fill 2
D G Cadd9 G D
Rec - ord - man.) do you real - ly think I can? If
w/Rhy. Fig. 1 (6 times)
w/Fill 2
G Cadd9 G D G Cadd9 G
not for the mon - ey and not for the show, are you here for me or here
w/Fill 2
D G Cadd9 G D
for the dough? Mis - ter Rec - ord - man,
(Mis - ter Rec - ord - man.) do you
G Cadd9 G D G Cadd9 G
real - ly give a damn? Mis - ter Rec - ord - man,
(Mis - ter
w/Fill 2
D G Cadd9 G D
Rec - ord - man.) do you real - ly think I can? Mis - ter
Freely
G
Rec - ord - man.
let ring